A John Catt Publication

The 10 STEP GUIDE to ACING EVERY EXAM you ever take

Lucy Parsons

First Published 2017

by John Catt Educational Ltd,
12 Deben Mill Business Centre, Old Maltings Approach,
Melton, Woodbridge IP12 1BL

Tel: +44 (0) 1394 389850 Fax: +44 (0) 1394 386893
Email: enquiries@johncatt.com
Website: www.johncatt.com

ISBN: 978 1 911382 19 5

Set and designed by Theoria Design Ltd

Foreword

Cookies. Those frustrating little internet security things that track our history and practically stalk us, without us even noticing; we all hate them, it seems. However, they're not all that bad – they can filter our searches and newsfeeds to make content more applicable to what we search and view most often. In my case, it was this world of internet cookies that lead me to Lucy Parsons.

Lucy's Facebook page, Life More Extraordinary, was a recommended advert in my feed and, let me tell you this, having found Lucy suddenly made all those useless hours of scrolling through Facebook and procrastinating, well, frankly, a little less useless, as a vast understatement.

What drew me in to Lucy was her brash and seemingly overconfident claim, that what she had to say would change my life. With it, I could live the life I envisaged and achieve all of my academic dreams. I am always hesitant whenever anyone makes a haughty statement like that. So naturally, I had to check it out.

If you take anything from this foreword, let it be this: I was enormously wrong. It's not an arrogant claim if it's true. Whatever level of education you are in, whatever subjects you are studying, if you follow Lucy's steps and implement her methods, it will totally alter your way of thinking and your attitude towards work, but not least your grades and academic success. My grades are proof; I got a sheet of paper last August telling me I had achieved 10 *A**s and 2 *A*s in my GCSEs. I had hassled many of my friends to check out Life More Extraordinary and go and work with Lucy in the year or so leading up to exams, but those who weren't willing to listen to the 10-step key to success were invariably the same of my friends who were disappointed on results day.

Keep in mind that there is no magic 'hack' to school; that's not what Lucy offers. It's about you; you have to be willing to listen, take this on board, and put the effort in. You have to be willing to read this book, cover to cover, and take action. I feel so lucky to have just stumbled across this remarkable lady but even more fortunate that I decided that day, on a whim, that I would confront her brash claims. Thank God for cookies.

Laura Jane Baxter
A-Level student, Kent

For all the ambitious dreamers who deeply value education

To Andy, thank you for supporting me in all that I do

To Iris and Wilf, one day I hope this book will help you too

To Valerie, a talented teacher and wonderful friend who was taken from this world before she had given all she had to give

Contents

Introduction

It was a crisp February morning when the idea for this book first came into my head. I was busy in my morning routine, getting my children ready for school, but the idea hit in a flash of inspiration. I'd heard various people saying that you should focus on teaching what you're better at than most other people and I knew in an instant what I was better at: taking exams, getting excellent results and not driving myself insane with stress in the process.

By the time I'd dropped my children off that morning I pretty much had a complete outline for the book in my head. I came home and started writing; I had written a chapter before lunchtime.

Within eight days, I'd completed the first version of this book and within a few more weeks it was for sale on my website as a PDF.

Over the following year or so many students came to my website to read my blog and they ended up buying my book. I had wonderful feedback and many messages of thanks letting me know how my approach to taking exams had helped others. Just under a year after the book had initially gone on sale, Alex Sharratt, Managing Director of John Catt Educational Ltd, was directed to my website by my friend Leah Stewart. He downloaded the free chapter of the book that I offered to readers and next morning he sent me an email offering me the chance to publish the book with them.

It had always been my dream to have a properly published book and I couldn't believe how easily the opportunity had presented itself to me.

The version of the book you will read here is considerably different from the one I originally self-published. In the 18 months between writing the first version and sitting down to write this one, I learned a lot and that learning is included in this book. From reading books, talking to others, listening to and helping my clients and blog readers and reflecting on my own experiences I have been able to add a lot of valuable insight and information. This is mainly in the first three chapters, or steps, in this version of the book. However, I have come to realise how utterly essential these three chapters are as a foundation for success for any ambitious student.

The purpose of this book is to give you a clear step-by-step plan for getting truly excellent grades in any exam you might take. My approach is transferable to any school level exam, and works largely for exams of all types at any level of education. Every piece of advice that you follow in this book will take you closer to getting the very best exam grades possible for you.

Now, I know as well as anyone else, that exam grades are not the be-all and end-all of life. However, for many, many young people they're a very important step on their road to achieving their hopes and dreams. Excellent exam grades open doors for you and it's my desire that you shall get the necessary grades to push open every door that you wish to go through.

However, there is also a deeper lesson in all of this. Studying for exams has been one of the most profound experiences of my life in terms of personal development. Through determination and hard work, I have found reserves of mental strength and grit that I never knew I had. I have also learned to use my brain in ever more subtle, creative and analytical ways. I hope you will discover and develop similar things within yourself as you work your way through your education.

Right from the beginning I intended this book to be immensely practical and helpful. For that reason, there are many exercises that you should take seriously if you want to get the most out of the book. Without doing the exercises you will miss the majority of the benefits of reading the book. To make it easier for you, I've created a companion workbook to go alongside this book which you can download for free from my website. You can find it at www.lifemoreextraordinary.com/workbook. I would encourage you to download it before you start reading so that you can fill in the exercises as you go along.

You should be aware that this book wasn't created in a vacuum. Throughout my life many, many people have played a supporting role in helping me to discover the lessons I'm about to share with you. The first and most notable are my parents; they have been entirely supportive of my education and done everything in their power to help me to achieve my dreams. I can't thank them enough. Then there are the special teachers who have helped me. The ones who had the biggest impact on me were: Mr Jones, my primary school headteacher; Mr Hill, who taught me humanities in Years 7 to 9; Mr Zammit, who was my form tutor in Years 7 to 9, and Mrs McVeigh who taught me English Literature in Year 12. Then there were my mentors in my first job, not in education, Roy Perticucci and Mike McNamara who drilled into me the disciplines of logical thinking and the clear presentation of ideas. Finally, there are the wise and worthy teachers who supported me through the early years of my teaching career: Liz Taylor, Steve Pallett, Fleur Spore, Fiona Stone and Izzy Roberts.

I would also like to thank my husband, Andy, for being utterly supportive of all my ideas and endeavours; I'm so lucky to be married to you. Iris and Wilf, thank you for being proud of your mummy for writing a book and sharing my happiness in my achievements. I hope I inspire you to forge your own paths and do meaningful work of your own in the future.

However, the biggest group of people I'd like to thank are the thousands of students who read my blog and emails every week and trust me to help them to achieve their hopes and dreams. You've all taught me so much and it's an honour to be allowed to help you with your education. My hope is that this book will help you, and many more readers like you, to get the absolute most out of your own years of learning.

So, without further ado, let's get started....

Part 1
Setting yourself up for success

The majority of advice on how to get excellent grades in exams starts, and ends, with the practical 'how to' stuff. However, what I've learned, from my own experience and from teaching others, is that there is some very important foundational work that needs to happen before you're ready for time management tips and working out how to revise.

Most of this foundational work is about getting your head in the right place to actually get on and do the work. Therefore, in the first three steps I'm going to help you get your head into the right place to succeed. You may really enjoy this work which involves a lot of self-reflection. You might find it hard; this is a sure sign that this work is super important for you to do thoroughly, and to keep working on even after you've finished reading this book. On the other hand, you may read these chapters and think 'this is pointless, let's get to the practical stuff'. What I want to say to you now is that you need to keep an open mind and commit to completing the exercises in these steps as thoroughly as you are able. The rest of the advice, the more practical stuff, that I give in this book will be much less helpful and powerful unless your head is sorted and you're in the right mental place to push on through and implement what I advise, even when the going gets tough.

Let's lay the foundations of your exam success together.

Step 1
Your great big 'why'

'If you can dream it, you can do it.'
Walt Disney

This chapter includes:

- Why you need to know your great big 'why' before you start studying for your exams
- How to identify your great big 'why'
- How to identify your target grades as a result of knowing your great big 'why'

Let's start with a short, personal story.

I was nine years old and with my family on a day trip to Cambridge. As we walked along the cobbled streets and around the Great Court of Trinity College, I was awe-struck by the gravitas and grey beauty of the place. I can still remember the feel of the chilly East Anglian breeze on my cheeks in the moment that I knew, just knew, that I had to become a student at the University of Cambridge.

From that day on I did everything in my power to improve myself and shape myself into the prospective student I suspected Cambridge wanted. I exerted huge amounts of my own will and self-discipline. I voluntarily studied extra subjects for exams over and above all my contemporaries at school. I didn't get a part time job as a teenager so I could focus on my studies. I read the newspaper every day and focused on reading serious novels. The nine years between the day when I decided it was my dream to study at Cambridge and the day I took my last A Level exam when I was eighteen years old were entirely devoted to achieving my goal.

Why have I just told you this little personal story?

Well, it's to demonstrate to you the importance of having a wider vision and purpose to studying for your exams. My dream of studying at Cambridge kept me focused on getting grades that many might have thought were out of my reach. That dream kept me sitting at my desk studying through tiredness and migraines. It kept me there when I felt lonely because I knew other people my age were out having fun or my family were companionable together in the kitchen downstairs. It kept me going over revision notes over and over again to make sure all the facts, ideas and concepts were firmly entrenched in my head. It kept me focused on doing one more past paper just to make sure that I really knew my stuff.

In essence, without my dream I would have worked far less hard, been much less determined and a great deal less focused. I have no doubt that I would have achieved lower grades in both my GCSEs and my A Levels and done far fewer things in my spare time that would help me win a place at an outstanding university.

My dream became a part of my identity; I would tell teachers that I was going to study at Cambridge University before I had even taken my GCSEs. They would often look at me with a mixture of amusement, bewilderment and awe. I would also tell my parents' friends, who probably thought I was a bit up myself. Very occasionally, I'd tell one of my friends or peers, but most of the time this was a bit too risky even for me because of the potential for opening myself up to mockery. The thing was, I was making this dream a part of who I was. I was making it real in my own head. For me, it would destroy who I was if I didn't make it come true. This made the stakes incredibly high; I had to do everything in my power to make it come true.

I hope you'll be happy to hear that all my hard work and self-sacrifice paid off. I did well at GCSE getting four A*s, six A's and a B. This was well enough for Cambridge to ask me for interview when I applied. However, I really excelled myself at A Level and earned five A grades. This was more than enough to secure the conditional place that Cambridge had offered me.

So, what can you learn from my experience?

You need a dream, a vision or a purpose for your studies. You need to know your great big 'why', the reason why you're taking these exams and what door they are opening for you.

Without this dream, vision or purpose you won't go that extra mile and stretch yourself to get stunningly good exam results. You won't force yourself to keep studying even when you feel under the weather or tired. You won't pick yourself up, dust yourself off and get back to the books when you've had a setback. The dream is what sustains you through all the difficult times. It motivates you when you'd rather be doing something else and gives you the will power that you need to just keep going.

'A dream doesn't become reality through magic; it takes sweat, determination and hard work.'
Colin Powell

What's your great big 'why'?

I've said enough about me. Now it's over to you. You need to work out what your great big why is so that it can be the guiding light and force behind all the work you need to do to get the best grades possible. I'm going to show you how to do this.

Before we start though I'll just give you a word to the wise. Your great big 'why' doesn't have to be as grandiose as mine. You don't have to decide at the age of nine that you want to study at Cambridge (if you're reading this it's probably already a little bit too late for that anyway). Your vision is allowed to be relatively modest in the general scheme of things or, you can have grander and more important ambitions than me (do you fancy saving the world?!). The size of your dream doesn't matter. What matters is that it rings true to you and really speaks to your heart. You have to be genuinely hungry for it and have a strong vision of what it will look like in your future. Don't, whatever you do, try to borrow someone else's dream, whether that's your parents', your siblings', your friends' or someone famous. Your dream has to be your own or this stuff won't work.

Now you've understood that, let's get on with the important work. We need to know your great big 'why'.

Start here

You're about to do some deep thinking. I'm going to ask you some questions and I want you to go as deep as you possibly can into your heart's desires to answer these questions honestly and truthfully.

To make this exercise as powerful as possible I believe it's best to write your answers down. There's something about writing things, rather than simply thinking them, that makes your thoughts and ideas more concrete and helps you to think more in depth. You can download the special accompanying workbook from lifemoreextraordinary.com/workbook to write down your answers to these questions, as well as all the other exercises in this book.

Are you ready to get all deep and meaningful? Good, let's go.

Exercise: Your great big 'why'

1. When you look five or ten years into the future, after you've finished your education, what kind of life do you want to live?
What kind of house do you want to live in? What kind of job do you want to be doing? What does your social life look like? Are you married? Do you have children? Do you have pets? What kind of car do you drive (or do you ride a bike instead)? What books do you read and what kinds of films do you watch? What do you do on a Sunday? Describe your answers to these questions in as much detail as possible.

2. Describe a typical day in the life of your ideal you in ten years' time.
What does your daily nitty gritty look like? Write down as much detail as you can.

3. Why are you attracted to this life?
What makes it exciting, fulfilling or something to aim for?

4. What do you want to achieve in your life?
Do you want a nice house and two children? Or, do you want to be prime minister? Or both? Maybe you'd rather be the scientist who comes up with the technological solution to global warming? Or you want to run your own business and be rich? What is it that you want to achieve?

5. What do you want to be admired for?
The way you bring up your children, your positive outlook and cheerful company or your positive influence on thousands of people's lives? Describe in detail what it is that you want to be admired for.

6. What mark do you want to leave on the world?
Maybe you want to write a book, invent a new technology, improve your community for the better or have happy, well-functioning children that contribute positively to society. This is how you're going to be remembered.

You may have found that there was some repetition and overlap between your answers to these questions. If you found that, it's a good thing. The more you repeat yourself, or the more often you see a theme coming through, the more strongly you can identify that it is a strong motivation for you and part of your true dream.

What will it take to achieve your dream?

Once you know what you're aiming for in life you need to understand how to get there. It's all very well if you know you want to go to Paris but if you've got no idea which way to go, what transport to use, how much it's going to cost and what you're going to need to take with you then going to Paris is just going to remain a dream.

So, you're going to have to do some research but don't worry, I'll break it down for you so you know what you need to find out.

When I decided that I wanted to go to Cambridge I understood that I would need to get truly excellent grades in all my exams. However, I was intimidated and ignorant about what else I would need to do and master in order to get there. I soon learned that the personal statement and interview were very important and that they'd be looking for someone who was an all-round high-achiever, who read widely and took an active part in the community. This meant that I started reading the newspaper every day, I kept taking music exams until I achieved Grade Eight on the oboe and I did things in my own community and in school. I also made sure I would get the maximum support for applying to Cambridge by moving to a school for my A Level studies that was more experienced in getting people into Oxbridge.

Your path to your dream

1. What is your dream?
Describe it in a couple of sentences.

2. If your dream is a lifestyle, how much do you think it's going to cost?
This is how much you're going to need to earn. What job could you do that will help you earn this much money? Would you be happy doing this job? What qualifications do you need to do this job? Do you need to go to university or college? What grades do you need to get in there? What other experience do you need to get on to that course?

3. Is your dream a particular job or career?
What do you need to do to get into that career? What qualifications do you need to do this job? Do you need to go to university or college? What grades do you need to get in there? What other experience do you need to get onto that course?

4. Is your dream going to a particular university or studying a certain subject?
What grades do you need in your exams to get into that university or onto that course? What other experience do you need, such as work experience or activities? Do you need to do any further reading or

independent research work in order to get onto that course or into that university?

Within 30 minutes of searching on Google, I'm sure you'll find many of the answers to these questions. What you can't find out from the internet you may have to ask experts in the field. For example, if your dream is to be a barrister you might need to get work experience with a barrister, or just have a coffee with one, and ask them all your questions. Over time you'll build up a more and more detailed picture of how to make your dream life happen and you can build those action steps into your plan.

However, the key thing you need to know at the moment is what grades you need to get in your school exams to open the doors to your dream life. These grades are your target grades. Write them down and make it your mission to achieve them, because they are your passport to your dream. When you're feeling unfocused, de-motivated and like studying is the last thing in the world that you want to be doing just remind yourself of your dream and get back to the books.

'Don't expect people to understand your grind when God didn't give them your vision.'
Unknown

Keep your dream front and centre of your mind

Once you know what your dream is it's a good idea to keep it front and centre of your mind and your life. There are various things you can do to make this happen.

1. Create yourself a vision board
Find pictures that represent your dream and stick them onto an A3 piece of paper (or larger). For me, my vision board would have had lots of pictures of Cambridge colleges and Cambridge life to keep me focused and motivated on what I wanted to achieve. If your dream is a house in the country, four children and a job that pays

for it all then find a picture of the kind of house you'd like to live in, a picture of a family of six and other pictures that represent the details of the life you'd like to live. Make it a living, breathing vision by adding pictures, quotes or meaningful scraps over time. Make it work for you.

2. Write a journal entry
You could write a journal entry describing your dream life, or an ideal day in your dream life, if you are more of a word person than a picture person. Fill it with detail like the clothes you're wearing, the people you're meeting, the things you're talking about and thinking about. Make it rich, colourful and enticing. Again, add to this over time. Re-write paragraphs and add in details or quotes as your learn more about the detail of your dream life.

Whenever you're struggling to motivate yourself to study look at your dream board or read your journal entry and visualise your dream life. For a couple of minutes, bask in the juicy visualisation of this amazing life that you're aiming for. Then, get back to the real-world and your studies so that you can make this dream life your future reality.

Bonus tip
If possible try to experience your dream life. For me, towards the end of the summer holidays every year my mum, sister and I usually visited Cambridge to do our back to school stationery shop. Not only did we buy pens, pencils, folders and dividers but we had time to wonder around the colleges soaking up the atmosphere. This was particularly powerful for me because it enabled me to even more strongly visualise myself in that environment and make it seem even closer to being a reality for me.

Where could you go and what could you do to experience your dream for real? Maybe you could go on a university summer school, do work experience or go and stand outside the kind of house you'd like to live in. Seeing it, living it and breathing it, even for only a few short minutes makes your dreams feel so much closer within your reach.

'Go after your dream no matter how unattainable others think it is.'
Unknown

Chapter summary

- Identify your great big why. Not for a second would I suggest that everyone should make their chosen destination Cambridge University; it's not for everyone, but you must have some idea of your ideal future in your head. Use the questions in this chapter to identify your dream.
- Take ownership of your dream and turn it into a plan. Find out what it will take to achieve your dream and create an action plan. It's particularly important that you know what grades you'll need to achieve your dream. These grades should be your target grades, in your head, not some data-generated grades that come from school. Write down the grades you'll need to achieve your dream and take ownership of them as your target grades.
- Visualise your dream very regularly, but particularly when you're feeling discouraged, disheartened or lacking motivation. Keep your vision board somewhere that you'll see it all the time. Tuck your journal entry into your planner or keep it in the notes app on your phone so you can look at it when you're on the bus or when you're waiting for a lesson to start. Whenever possible, experience your dream for real.
- Pour your heart and soul into the journey. You need to live and breathe your desire to reach your destination every day. It takes guts and determination to set your heart on something and make it the focus of all your activities, knowing that there is always the possibility of failure. Others won't always believe in you or your vision, so be the brave soul who lives their life reaching for their dreams.

- Take all the help and advice you can get. No one gave me a road map showing me how to get to Cambridge; I worked out the major milestones and obstacles along the way (mainly exam results, university applications and the dreaded interview). I then gleaned all the advice and clues I could on how to swing these things in my favour. It was like gathering clues in a mammoth treasure hunt and putting them all together to come up with the answer. Listen to anyone who's willing to give you some advice to help you along the way. Read articles and books and watch TV programmes, all of it will give you practical help as well as inspiration.
- Take responsibility for your own hopes and dreams. So many people will want to help you, even more will want to give you advice, but, ultimately only you can make your dreams come true. Take responsibility for your journey today and, with a fair wind, you will reach your dream destination.

Step 2
The mindset for success

> *'Whether you think you can or think you can't, you're right.'*
> Henry Ford

This chapter includes:

- Why believing in the power of effort and hard work will create your path to exam success
- How to combat your fear of failure
- Why you need to get out of your comfort zone to succeed
- Why you need to develop a mindset of self-belief and reject failure as an option

Your beliefs are powerful, particularly your beliefs about yourself and your own capabilities. As Henry Ford said in the quote above, you think yourself into success or into failure. It's your choice. If you choose to believe in yourself and choose to think the thoughts that support and nourish your belief in yourself, you put yourself in the mindset of success. If you choose to doubt your abilities and think negative thoughts about your chances of achieving your dreams, you're setting yourself up for failure.

Passing exams isn't rocket science, although rocket scientists tend to do pretty well in their exams. Getting the top grades is not the preserve of geniuses. I assure you that it is possible to get the grades you need and desire by digging deep and finding the inner resources necessary to do the work and learn the skills that you need. You just have to believe that you have it inside yourself and keep digging and searching until you find it.

When you believe that effort is the key ingredient for success and that failure is good because it's an opportunity to learn and improve, then you are on the right course to succeed in your exams. As Carol Dweck said: 'it's not always the people who start out the smartest who end up the smartest.'

Think about that for a minute and really let it sink in. Did you have classmates at primary school who seemed to find things easy but are now doing just averagely? Have you ever noticed a friend who plods along doing OK but then starts to put the effort in and you see their achievements soar?

It's possible to see this kind of thing in the sporting world. The tennis player Novak Djokovic spent the early years of his career doing pretty well, however when he decided to get really serious about his game his career soared. The effort he put in off the court really paid off on the court. I seriously believe that with the right effort applied in the right way anyone can improve their grades.

The rest of this book will be about how to exert the right effort in the right way. The rest of this chapter is about getting your mindset right; without having the right mindset, or belief in your ability to improve through effort, you will not fully realise the benefits of the practical advice I'm going to give later on.

This belief, that you can improve any basic quality that you possess through effort, is known as the growth mindset. The essence of the growth mindset is summed up in this quote:

> *'The passion for stretching yourself and sticking to it, even (or especially) when it's not going well, is the hallmark of the growth mindset.'*
> - Carol Dweck

If you keep pushing yourself and stretching yourself to learn and improve then over time you will become better at whatever you set your mind to. Stop trying to prove yourself over and over again and start trying to find the fun in learning; it's so much more interesting and enjoyable being a learner than someone who tries to prove themselves, it is also profoundly rewarding. Forget about the pride of getting the top grades in your exams. The satisfaction you get from exerting the effort to improve day-by-day, week-by-week and month-by-month is profound. It's this journey of self-discovery that will give you the courage and even deeper self-belief to achieve even greater things in the future.

The fear of failure

No matter how much effort you put in or how much you believe in yourself the fear of failure can still haunt you like a dark and forbidding shadow.

The fear of failure can sabotage even the smartest people with the brightest futures ahead of them. One client told me the story of how she earned the maths prize and an A* in Year 12 and was aiming to study maths at Cambridge, however the fear of failure hit her in Year 13 and she stopped working. She was scared about what it would say about her if she worked hard and didn't make the grades. She couldn't cope with the idea that her effort would not be rewarded. You can probably guess the end of the story, her grades took a nosedive and she didn't end up studying at Cambridge. She had to reapply to university and continued to struggle to find the resolve to study and carried on failing exams; she came to me to help her to break this vicious negative cycle.

If the fear of failure is holding you back from success you need to understand why you fear failure and address the root cause head on.

> *'Promise me you'll always remember: You're braver than you believe, and stronger than you seem, and smarter than you think.'*
> A.A. Milne

Answer these questions as thoroughly and deeply as you can. Write long answers that are as honest as possible. If you struggle to do this on your own, get someone else to ask you the questions and probe more deeply so that you realise the truth. Remember, you will find a printable copy of these questions in the downloadable workbook that accompanies this book. Get your copy at www.lifemoreextraordinary.com/workbook.

1. Does failing make you worry about what other people will think of you?
Are you worried about letting down your mum and dad if you don't get the grades they want you to? Are you worried about your friends laughing at you if you don't get the grades you're predicted? What is it that makes you so scared of what other people think?

2. Does failing make you worry about your ability to pursue the dream you identified in chapter 1?
Are you worried about not getting the grades you need to get into the university that's offered you a place? What about worrying you won't get the grades you need to get into sixth form? How much does your identity and the meaning of your life hinge on getting the grades you need?

3. Does failing make you worry that people will lose interest in you?
What if all your friends are cleverer than you and predicted to get much better grades? They've all got offers at Russell Group universities and you're headed for a university that's not so well respected. You've been friends since you were eleven but you can't see how they'd still want to be friends with you if you're clearly not a high-flyer like them. What other insecurities do you have that make you think that people like you for your cleverness?

4. Does failing make you worry about how clever you are?
You're worried that a poor set of exam results will make people think you're stupid for the rest of your life. Writing your lack-lustre GCSE grades on every application form from now until eternity makes you feel sick. Do your grades really show your value as a person?

5. Does failing make you worry about disappointing people whose opinion you value?
Maybe there's a teacher you really admire or your grandad has always believed in you, supported you and encouraged you more than anyone else throughout your life. You're desperate not to let them down because you know what the disappointment on their face will look like and you can anticipate the hollow feeling in your stomach when you see it. Do you really think that these people will stop liking you, loving you and believing in you because of what happened one day in an exam hall?

6. Do you play down your abilities and ambitions when you're talking to other people so that they don't expect too much from you?
You keep telling people that there's no way you'll get the straight As that school has predicted and you're really not that clever. What message are you giving to yourself when you say these kinds of things out loud to other people?

7. If, and when, you get a disappointing result, do you find it difficult to imagine what you could have done differently to get a better result?
You've got your mock exam grades back and got much worse grades than you wanted. You tell yourself that your expectations of yourself were too high and that you're meant to get low grades, instead of really digging deep into what you could have done differently so you can learn from your mistakes and do better next time. Why do you give up on yourself so easily?

8. Do you often get last-minute headaches, stomach aches, anxiety attacks, panic attacks or other physical or psychological symptoms that prevent you from completing your revision or doing your best in an exam?
What is it that you're trying to avoid? Are you looking for an excuse for failure?

9. Do you displace the tasks that are most important for helping you to achieve your dreams with things that will sabotage your preparation?
You hide from the important work you need to do by doing 'busy'

non-urgent work like tidying your room or phoning a friend just to put it off and distract yourself. If you're really honest with yourself you know what you're doing and could stop yourself if you really wanted to. Why do you do this?

10. Do you procrastinate and 'run out of time' to complete your homework tasks and revision properly?
You procrastinate over the things you should be doing and purposefully run out of time so that you sabotage your own results. What message are you trying to send to the world and to yourself when you do this?

Now you've answered these questions as honestly as possible you've probably uncovered some uncomfortable truths about how you're letting the fear of failure sabotage your pursuit of your dreams.

Now, I don't want you to to beat yourself up about your past thought patterns and behaviour. You can't change the past so be kind to yourself. Instead, I want you to forgive yourself and make a promise to yourself that you're going to move forward, from this moment, in a more positive and productive way.

Say out loud to yourself 'I forgive myself for sabotaging my own success in the past. From today onwards I will only do what supports my own success.'

One simple decision

Now that you've forgiven yourself for the things you've done in the past that were destructive to your own success you have one simple decision to make:

Are you going to succeed?

That may sound like a ridiculous question to ask. However, many people's response will be 'Well, I'll try,' or, 'I'll do my best.' These answers aren't good enough. The answer you're looking for is a resounding 'Yes!'

"What if, just in case, and I'll try are what you say when you believe failure is an option.'
PUSH, Chalene Johnson

You may be thinking to yourself, how on earth can I be certain that I'm going to succeed? There are all sorts of things that could go wrong. Well, I'm here to tell you that that is completely the wrong attitude. When you are hungry enough for your dream and you want to see it come true so badly that it hurts you will decide to succeed, you will believe in yourself and you will put the effort in to make it happen.

This is a smart decision because failure is no longer an option. Your only option is to find out how to succeed and make it happen.

Making this decision is a very simple but incredibly powerful thing to do. It's a decision that happens inside you but it reaches down into the depths of who you really are. When you're walking down the street most people won't be able to tell that you've made this decision. However, when your nearest and dearest next see you they'll recognise a change in your energy and a shift in your attitude. They perhaps won't know quite what it is yet, but they'll soon start seeing the results. If strangers were to stop and look at you they would see something that was making you stand taller and look about you with more confidence, but they wouldn't be able to say what made you different from other people. But, you'll know. You'll know that you've made this decision and, for you, it has changed everything.

So, let me ask you again:

Are you going to succeed?

Good. Let's move on.

Getting out of your comfort zone

Now that you've decided to succeed, believe in yourself and do whatever it takes to achieve your dreams you'll constantly be pushing yourself. Every day you will have to stretch yourself beyond what you're comfortable doing and try unfamiliar and difficult things.

You may find yourself resistant to this.

A client of mine declared to me a year ago that she wanted to study physical natural sciences at Cambridge. She was in the early stages of Year 12, doing all the right subjects and was clearly passionate about the subject matter of the course she wanted to study. A year later she'd received her AS results, she'd done very well in maths but her chemistry grade was particularly disappointing.

I asked her what had gone wrong with chemistry, we talked for a bit and eventually she told me: 'Maths is easy. I just have to remember a method and use it over and over again. For chemistry I actually have to revise, and remember stuff, and I don't know how to do that. It's outside my comfort zone.'

This girl was incredibly resistant to getting outside her comfort zone and finding a way that worked for her to learn and revise her chemistry. I left her saying: 'If you still want to pursue your dream you're going to have to get outside your comfort zone. If you don't want to do that you can forget your dream today.'

It's hard talk but it's the truth.

The beautiful thing is that when you push yourself outside your comfort zone what you used to find hard becomes easy. Your comfort zone shifts and that's when you start to feel the profound sense of satisfaction that comes from personal growth. There is nothing more rewarding than feeling the boundaries of your own possibilities expand inside yourself because of the effort you've applied to getting outside your comfort zone.

So, make a commitment to yourself today to always be reaching outside your comfort zone to see what more you can accomplish.

> *'As you move outside your comfort zone, what was once unknown and frightening becomes the new normal.'*
> Robin S. Sharma

No more excuses

The only person who loses out when you make excuses for yourself is you. Whether you're telling yourself you're not clever enough to get the top grades, not posh enough to go to Oxford, not rich enough to go to university, not hard working enough to do A Levels, you're making an excuse for yourself. Not only that but you're imposing your own artificial limits on your achievement.

From now on there is no excuse; you are in this, heart and soul, to succeed. You've decided that success is your only option, you've said that you believe in yourself so forget the excuses. Now is your time to shine. Unleash the deep power that is within you and let nothing get in your way.

Overcoming the doubters

Sometimes, no matter how much you believe in yourself and no matter how hard you work others don't believe in you. One of my blog readers wrote to me and said this:

'My science teacher thinks that I won't reach a C. It's really put me down to think that I can't pass and it's made me give up on revising science all together. I feel like I'm not getting any support from my teacher since they said that. Do you have any tips on how I can stay positive and not give up?'

This is what you need to do to overcome the doubters and prove them wrong. Show them what you're really made of and what you can do despite their lack of belief or lack of support.

Do this for you

At the end of the day, your exam results are for you and no one else. You're not doing this for your science teacher, your mum and dad or your pet goldfish. You're doing this for yourself. Your grades are going to help you get into sixth form or university, help you get a job in the future and give you self-esteem and self-respect. Most importantly, they are one step on the road to achieving your vision for your dream life. You may please other people or make them proud with your grades, but they're not going to change anyone else's life but yours.

Know what you're aiming for

Even if everyone around you seems to be sabotaging your attempts to get good grades, if you keep in mind what you're aiming for it will really help to keep you on track. You identified your great big why in chapter 1. Keep that dream in mind and it will help you to keep on track. This chapter has been all about mindset. *Your* mindset. You have to believe in yourself and your abilities before anyone else will. Show them, by example, that you're worthy of their belief.

In the workbook you'll find some positive mantras to repeat daily to instil your belief in your power and the inevitability of your success. Choose the mantra that speaks to you most clearly, or make up your own, and say it until you truly believe it.

Chapter Summary

- Your beliefs are powerful. Whatever you tend to believe about yourself, and tell yourself in your own internal dialogue, tends to come true. So start believing in yourself and telling yourself that you can do this thing, from this success will follow.
- Effort leads to personal growth. The trick is to apply this effort intelligently and we'll talk about how to do that in the following chapters.
- Forgive yourself for sabotaging your own success in the past. The fear of failure makes us do strange things, things that make us more likely to fail. Recognise your own past behaviour patterns and make a pact with yourself to improve them over time.
- Decide to succeed. It's a seemingly simple and small decision but it will be the catalyst for massive change in your outlook, effort and results.
- Get outside of your comfort zone. Do it regularly and watch the boundaries of your possibilities expand.
- Stop making excuses. You're a success now, you no longer need excuses.
- Believe in yourself and you'll prove the doubters wrong.

Step 3
Look after yourself

As you consciously choose to give yourself the gifts of self-care, they become an integral part of your rhythm and the vital tools that you will tap into for the rest of your life.'
A Woman's Truth: A Life Truly Worth Living,
Miranda J. Barrett

This chapter includes:

- How to look after yourself so you're in the best of mental and physical health to support your studies

While you're studying for your exams hour-by-hour, day-by-day and week-by-week you need to make time to look after yourself. Studying done well is more like a marathon than a sprint; the tortoise, not the hare, will win out in the end. Like any athlete you need to follow a training plan that will lead you to success and an integral part of this is treating your body, your mind and your soul with respect and tender loving care.

In my work with young people one of the things that makes me most sad is when I hear about mental or physical ill-health impacting their life chances. I get emails all the time from young people suffering from severe anxiety, depression, eating disorders and physical illnesses that have forced them to take time off school and reduced the amount of time they can spend on their studies at home.

You have one body, one mind and one life. It is your responsibility to treat each of these things with the love, care and respect that it deserves. If you do this, your body and mind will reward you in return by supporting you in your attempts to reach your goals. Without your health your dreams are just wishes drifting away from you like clouds in the sky.

So, how do you look after your mind, body and soul so that they can support you in the pursuit of your dreams?

Sleep well

"Rest when you're weary. Refresh and renew yourself, your body, your mind, your spirit. Then get back to work."
Ralph Marston

The foundation of a healthy life is getting good quality sleep every night, and enough of it. Sleep is really important for learning. It's when your brain let's all that new information sink in so that it sticks, creating new neural pathways in your brain, while nothing else is being demanded of it. If you cheat yourself of sleep you're lowering the return on the hard-work of studying you've done during the day. Sleep isn't just important for your learning, however; it protects you from illness, repairs injuries and makes you more likely to be a cheerful person. For all these reasons, you really can't afford to skimp on sleep.

The first step is working out roughly how much sleep you think that you need. Most adults will need seven to eight hours per night. Some may need more. Experiment with how much sleep you get and how it makes you feel in your body, your mood and how well your brain works taking on and understanding new information.

Once you know how much sleep you need the next step is working out what you need to do to get a good night's sleep. You probably need to stop stimulating your mind at least an hour before you plan to go to sleep. That means stop studying at least an hour before bedtime. What activities could you do that wind you down and relax you in the last hour of the day? Some ideas include:

- Spending some time with family members
- Watching your favourite programme on TV
- Reading a gentle book that you find enjoyable and not too stimulating (I made the mistake of trying to read *Middlemarch* during my A Level revision period and it really didn't give my brain a rest)
- Having a bath
- Talking to a friend on the phone; but only if that friend will keep you in a positive frame of mind, make you laugh or be supportive. Don't vent your exam stress on someone who's in the same position as you, it's not kind.
- Taking the dog for a late-night walk
- Meditating
- Doing gentle exercise like a bedtime yoga sequence

There are also things that you shouldn't be doing in that last hour before bed:

- Drinking tea or coffee
- Looking at a screen on your phone, tablet or computer (the light they give off is highly stimulating to the brain)
- Doing very vigorous exercise
- Having an argument or doing something else that makes you upset

You know yourself better than anyone. Find out what your optimum wind-down activities are so that you can get the best night's sleep possible. You may also find that if you don't exercise your body as much as your brain during the day you don't sleep well.

Exercise well

Exercise works wonders for your mental and physical health. If you're feeling stressed or worried about something going for an energetic run or doing an all-consuming yoga session can really take your mind off it and put it into perspective. Doing half an hour of exercise each day can also improve the quality of your sleep because it makes your body as well as your brain tired.

Movement and exercise also help you to concentrate. So, when you're studying make sure every 30-60 minutes you stand up, move away from your desk and do some stretches or walk around the house (in Step 9 there's a whole list of suggestions for active study or revision breaks). This will re-invigorate your brain by giving it a rest and getting your blood moving. You'll be fresher and more receptive to new information when you get back to your studies

Make sure that exercise is a part of your life. You will feel the benefits of it in your mental and physical health as well as your studies. You have always got time to exercise.

> *'To keep the body in good health is a duty... otherwise we shall not be able to keep our mind strong and clear.'*
> Buddha

Eat and drink well

I'm sure you're always hearing messages about how to eat and drink healthily and you really don't need another person ramming this stuff home. I'm still going to say my little piece, but I'll keep it short.

Try to eat good food while you're studying; your body and mind will thank you for it in the long run. What do I mean by good food? Aim for at least five portions of fruit and veg per day, and more if you can manage it. Try to keep fast food, very sugary and fatty foods to a minimum. Also, don't let your body rely on stimulants like caffeine. It's much better to drink lots of water and have fresh fruit or nuts for your snacks than a can of cola and a chocolate bar. You may get a quick lift from the cola and chocolate but it won't last in your blood stream the way water and fruit will.

The other big thing is to eat a good breakfast full of slow-release energy and nutrition that will keep you sustained until lunchtime. Good examples are: porridge with fruit, a green juice, fruit smoothie or an omelette with some vegetables. I have found in my own life that when you're trying to build good habits into your life, such as eating more fruit and veg, the earlier in the day you get those habits in the more likely you are to succeed. So, make healthy food part of your breakfast and you'll start each day as you mean to go on.

Make it easy for yourself to drink plenty of water by carrying a water bottle with you at all times. You'll be less tempted to grab a coffee if you've got water with you (and you'll save some money too!).

I'm no healthy living guru but I have done work on improving my health and fitness and it makes a massive difference to how you feel physically and psychologically. You will feel healthier and happier throughout the period when you're studying for and taking your exams if you try to put into place some, if not all, of the things I've mentioned here.

"Take care of your body. It's the only place you have to live."
Jim Rohn

Take time for yourself

One of the most important things in keeping a healthy outlook on life is to take time for yourself. When I'm working, I sometimes just go for a little walk around the garden to see how the plants are doing, or I walk around the block. This time isn't wasted time, it's recharge time; it gives you time to think, make new connections in what you're learning, or just rest your mind.

Other things you can do are sit quietly with your eyes closed, take a nice long bath or meditate. If you're more of an outgoing type of person, you may crave company. In which case, catch up with friends or spend some quality time with your family. You need to do whatever helps you to feel recharged and energized.

The secret to looking after yourself and staying energised throughout the day is finding the little pockets of time during the day when you can indulge and relax. For example, lunchtime at school might be the perfect time to catch up with friends and have a good chat. When you arrive home from school you can have a drink and a snack, chat to other family members who are at home, watch a TV programme or do some reading before you get on with your homework. The last hour of the day is a great time to treat yourself and relax.

When you look after yourself properly and give yourself the chance to recharge in the best way for you your appetite for learning will be that much greater because you're giving yourself the time, space and energy to make your learning count.

Part time jobs and extra-curricular activities

One of the most frequent questions that readers of my blog ask is how to balance the demands of a part-time job or their extensive out-of-school activities with their studies for school.

It's natural to want your own money so that you don't have to ask for it and you have plenty to pay for driving lessons or the clothes, shoes, concert tickets and hair products that you really want.

However, you really need to weigh up the importance of these things against your long term goals. How important is it to be able to buy a new top every month compared to getting into your first choice of university or having that high-profile career as a barrister?

When you're thinking about whether to get a part-time job or keep a part-time job the main consideration is how it's going to impact your grades. Some people manage to balance the two against each other very successfully, they find that the job provides a great contrast to their studies and they enjoy it and feel energised by it. However, if you get overly tired because of the demands of your job or it's preventing you from spending as much time as you should on your studies (or you're depriving yourself of sleep to get both done) then you probably need to cut the hours you spend on your job or write your resignation letter and leave.

This is all about balancing the needs of the future against the needs of the present. Making these kinds of decisions can really test your commitment to the dream, or great big why, that you discovered in chapter one. What I really want you to do is consider very deeply whether, in ten or 15 years' time, you will think you made a good decision to spend every Sunday stacking supermarket shelves rather than reaching your full potential in your studies.

As far as extra-curricular activities are concerned I would urge you to go for quality over quantity. What do I mean by this? Well, instead of trying to play the piano and the violin, be in the school orchestra, play for the school hockey team and volunteer in a charity shop every weekend you need to choose the things that matter most to you. What are you best at? What do you enjoy most? Which activities make you feel best about yourself and give you a real boost when you do them? These are the things to keep. It can be really hard to make these decisions, but you can always come back to some of the things you drop when you get to university or once you've finished university. Again, it's about the opportunity cost of deciding whether you want to do all these things now and possibly sacrifice your studies and your dream, or you want to go whole-heartedly after your ambition.

Of course, if you're getting the grades you want and need whilst holding down a part-time job, playing two instruments, being in the hockey team and getting enough sleep then I think you should carry on. But, if you're stressed, worn out and struggling those are sure signs that something needs to change and you need to make some difficult decisions about what to temporarily remove from your life.

Your plan to look after yourself

Answer these questions to come up with your plan for how to look after yourself so that you can do your best in your studies. There's a copy of these questions in the workbook which you can download from www.lifemoreextraordinary.com/workbook.

Sleep

1. Ideally, how many hours sleep do you need every night?

2. What time do you need to get up in the morning?

3. Knowing how much sleep you need and what time you need to get up in the morning, what time should you be turning your light out and going to sleep?

4. What activities help you to wind down and relax in the last hour of the day so that you're ready to calmly drift off to sleep? Write down your ideal last hour of the day here.

Exercise

1. What is your favourite type of exercise? List one to three types of exercise below.

2. When is the ideal time in your days or weeks to fit in these types of exercise?

Eat and drink

1. List your three favourite healthy snacks to carry with you.

2. How will you make sure you've always got a healthy snack to take with you? Who do you need to talk to? Do you need any packaging to help you carry them?

3. What's your favourite healthy breakfast? I challenge you to eat at least two portions of fruit or vegetables before you leave the house every morning. How are you going to make this happen?

Take time for yourself

1. What activities make you feel relaxed, recharged and rejuvenated? List at least five here.

2. How can you fit these activities into your everyday life or your week? What are the ideal times for you to do them?

Part-time jobs

1. If you have a part-time job how many hours per week does it take?

2. Do you feel that your grades would improve if you didn't have a part-time job? Why?

3. Are you willing to cut down your hours or leave your job to get better grades and pursue your dream?

Extra-curricular activities

1. List below all the extra-curricular activities that you do and how much time they take each week.

2. Do you feel that any of these activities are having a negative effect on your grades?

3. Which activities do you enjoy the most and give you the biggest boost?

4. Which activities are you willing to sacrifice to pursue your dream and get better grades?

Chapter Summary

- Looking after yourself is vital to getting the best grades. If you choose to sacrifice your mental or physical health then your grades will also suffer.
- Sleep is the cornerstone of good health and well-being. Identify how many hours of sleep you need every night to be cheerful, alert and happy and make a plan to make sure you get that sleep!
- Exercise is a great way to keep your mind fresh for your studies and to keep your body healthy. List out your favourite sorts of exercise and make a plan for how you're regularly going to fit them into your life.
- Eating healthily will help to keep your body healthy and your mind alert. Plan your healthy breakfasts and snacks to pack the vitamins in early in the day.
- Make sure you make time for yourself to relax, re-energise and think.
- Seriously consider whether there are any activities or obligations (like a part-time job) that are damaging your chances of getting the grades you need. If there are you need to make difficult decisions about which activities to keep and which you'd like to let go.

Section II
Do the Work

In this part of the book, we are moving on from how you set yourself up for success to how you actually make your amazing grades happen. This chapter is full of how-to tips, but you must have completed all the exercises in the previous three chapters if you want to be sure that you're going to follow through on the suggestions that follow. Without knowing your great big 'why', having the right mindset and having a strong foundation in terms of how you look after your mind and body you will find that your ability and will to follow these instructions are not as strong as they otherwise might be.

This chapter includes:

- How starting work today will set you up for the greatest success
- How to make a plan to get the work done
- How to get organised and stay on top of your work
- How to create good study habits that will sustain your success throughout the academic year

> *"The best preparation for tomorrow is to do today's work superbly well."*
> William Osler

Whether you've always been a diligent hard-worker, always striving to do your best in your studies, or you've picked this book up in a panic because your exams are getting frighteningly close and you know you should have invested more time and effort earlier in the course, I don't want you to worry.

It is never too late to start doing the work. On the other hand, it's never too early. So my main message here is to start today.

"To begin, begin."
William Wordsworth

What do I mean by 'doing the work'?

When you start studying for any course that ends with an exam, work will come your way. You may be in school where you sit in a classroom every day, the teacher teaches you stuff and sets you tasks that you do in school or at home. You may be at university where you spend much of your day reading in the library, some of the time attending lectures and some of the time in tutorials or supervisions with your lecturers. You may be doing a distance learning course where you get a box of books and documents and a list of tasks that you have to complete.

All of this is work.
The problem is that when you start a course, maybe two or even three years before the final exam, that exam feels a very long way away. Even for the most diligent amongst you, at the beginning of the course there can be the temptation to cut corners, or not put your best effort in. For example, you may know that it's a good idea to read through your class notes every day after school to make sure you understand them. However, you're planning to go out one evening, you've got important homework tasks to do before you go out and your mum needs you to do some chores around the house. Also, your exams are 18 months away so you don't read through your class notes when you get home from school. The next day this good habit doesn't seem so important anymore (because you didn't do it yesterday) so you let it slip thinking you'll catch up at the weekend. Before you know it, it's been a week or maybe even a month since you did this good habit. It's no longer a habit and there's too much to catch up on so you give up.

I get it. I've been there. We're all human. Acknowledge this and come up with a plan to tackle it.

Why is doing the work so important?
Doing the work as you go through the course is the cornerstone to your success. If you pay attention in lessons, do the classwork and homework to the best of your ability and hand it on in time, you're actually working in the most efficient way possible.

What I mean is, you have to be there in that classroom. Those hours of your life have been allotted to being in that location, with those classmates and with that teacher. The best thing you can do to get the most out of life is use that time wisely. And, by wisely, I mean paying attention and doing the tasks that are set.

Those hours in the classroom are the first time you come across the information you're consuming at that time, or learning the skill you're being taught. If you don't pay attention now you will have to do this all over again, at another point in time, probably with less encouragement and support.

With homework, it's always best to do it at the time it's set and hand it in on time. This is for two reasons:

1. Your teacher sets that particular piece of homework on that particular day for a good reason. That homework will generally be supporting what you learned in class that day, or leading up to something you'll be focussing on in class at some point in the near future. If you do that piece of homework within the time frame set by the teacher, it will reinforce what you've learned, fixing it in your brain so it will be easier to remember when you come back to it at revision time.
2. Hand it in on time; there's nothing worse than a backlog of work. I remember once, in my early days of secondary school, I let a backlog of homework build up. I did this deliberately. I just thought it was more fun to watch TV or play with my friends than to do the work. I was also having a hard time adjusting to the new routine of homework

demanded by the school. Suddenly, I realised that much of this homework was due in ASAP. I've always been a bit of a teacher pleaser and I couldn't think of anything worse than handing it in late and getting on the wrong side of all the teachers at my new school. So, for the next few days when I came home from school I had to sit down in a serious way, do homework and very little else except sleep and eat. In essence, it was miserable. I never let this happen to me again. You can live a more balanced, happy and healthy life if you keep on top of your deadlines and don't let them get on top of you.

The final thing I'll say on this, is that you should do the work to the best of your ability. This may sound a bit preachy and boring, but when it comes to revision time you'll thank yourself a thousand times for doing so.

There is nothing worse when you're revising than coming to a section of your original notes to find that they're, at best, a bit sketchy or, at worst, completely missing. Having a good quality first attempt at all the work in your course is the foundation for a successful exam period. This is also the best time to iron out any wrinkles in your understanding of the material in your course, talk to the teacher, and get feedback and extra input. Deal with the problems now; don't let them pile up for later.

Your plan to do the work, starting today

'Give me six hours to chop down a tree and I will spend the first four sharpening the axe.'
Abraham Lincoln

If you have been doing the work, you can paste a smug little look on your face and give yourself a metaphorical pat on the back, well done! However, if you haven't been doing the work I seriously hope that you're not feeling totally freaked out by now. The thing is, it's never too late to start doing the work. What you have to do is:

- Make a commitment to do the work from now on
- Make a plan for how you're going to make this happen

There are two steps you need to take to make your plan for how you're going to make this happen.

1. Organise your time
2. Organise your work

The next two chapters are going to help you to do these two things, whilst the final chapter in this section will talk about how you can create habits that help you to sustain your organisation and support your goals.

Step 4

How to manage your time

This chapter includes:

- How to make a plan to get the work done

> *'Time is our most valuable nonrenewable resource, and if we want to treat it with respect, we need to set priorities.'*
> Albert-László Barabási

Time management is the absolute foundation skill of any successful person. If you want to be a successful student and get amazing grades you are no exception; you need to learn to manage your time effectively.

When I was studying for my own GCSEs and A Levels time management was the cornerstone of my strategy. I set myself a weekly goal of how much time I would spend on my studies and I stuck to it, rigidly.

I'll give you an example. When I was studying for my A Levels, I planned out my week (outside school) like this. I would get home from school at 4pm. On Monday to Thursday I would then spend half an hour having a cup of tea and a snack, chatting to my mum and reading the newspaper. At 4:30pm I would go up to my bedroom and start work. I would work through until 6:30pm when my mum served our evening meal. At 7pm I would go back upstairs and continue working until 9pm. I would then come downstairs and watch TV for an hour before going up to bed to read for a bit before going to sleep.

I kept this routine going for the two years through which I was studying for my A Levels. It was hard work, I'm not going to lie to you, and took a lot of self-discipline and commitment, but I was rewarded with five A grades and my place at Cambridge, which was the dream I was trying to fulfil.

I still use this kind of approach to planning my time now. If you think about it, it's a bit like the principle of a school timetable. There is a time slot allotted for everything you do in your life. There's a time for sleeping, a time for relaxing, time for working etc. If you plan out your time like this you know you'll always get everything done, you know that you'll be prioritising achieving your dream over everything else that life might demand of you and you always know what you should be doing at any one point in time. If your mum starts nagging you to do homework you can say, 'Look at my timetable, mum, this is my break time. I'll get back to work at 7:30pm when my timetable says I will.' You never need to feel guilty about taking time off again because you've planned it and the clock will tell you if you've procrastinated for too long!

Create your own weekly study routine

I'm going to help you to create your own weekly study routine, like the one I followed while I was studying for my A Levels. Students that I've worked with have found this simple strategy incredibly helpful because it helps to keep them accountable whilst also, rather counter-intuitively, giving them freedom. You need to try it to see what they mean!

You will need an outline weekly routine (like the one shown at the end of this step) before you get started. There is a copy of this in the downloadable workbook which you can get from www.lifemoreextraordinary.com/workbook (with a link to download a version in Excel, ready for you to edit) if you'd prefer to save some time, or you can make your own in in a spreadsheet, word processor or by hand.

Essentially, you need to have the days of the week along one side and the twenty four hours of the day down the other side. You also need space for a key. If you're doing this exercise on paper rather than on the screen you will also need some coloured pens, pencils or highlighters.

What should be in your weekly routine?

1. Sleep

We've already talked about the importance of sleep if you want to be a successful student. In the section *Look after yourself*, you wrote down how much sleep you need every night and when you need to get up and go to bed to achieve this. So, the first thing I want you to add to your weekly routine is sleep. Colour in the hours you're going to be asleep and add that colour to the key.

2. Self-care time

Mark in the time at the beginning of the day and at the end of the day that you need for self-care. This includes getting up, washing, dressing and the reverse at the end of the day. You might also add in half-an-hour for a cup of tea and a snack when you get home from school. I call these times, when you're moving from one activity to another (school to home) transition times. You need to recognise the importance of transition times for you to adjust psychologically from one situation to another. Often, not allowing for transition time can lead to what we label as procrastination. However, it's actually a symptom of the fact that you haven't recognised that you need time and space for transition.

Colour in the hours you're going to use for self-care and transition times and add that colour to the key.

3. Meal-times at home

Mark off the times when your family regularly eats. When I was in the sixth form we ate at 6:30pm. I always took from 6:30pm until 7pm to eat, then I'd go back to the books. You will also want to mark in breakfast time.

Colour in the hours when you'll be eating and add that colour to the key.

4. School time and travel time

Colour in the hours when you're at school and when you're travelling to and from school and add that colour to the key.

5. Your interests, hobbies and part-time work

In step 3 I asked you to think seriously about your commitments to your part-time work and extra-curricular activities. Hopefully you've made some firm decisions about what you're going to keep doing and what you're going to stop doing.

On your routine, add in all the things you're going to continue doing outside school work. Make sure you've marked off the times when these things happen on a regular basis.

6. Exercise

Make sure you've allowed some time to move your body on a daily basis. Taking regular exercise helps your brain to work better and keeps you physically and mentally healthy.

Colour in the times when you'll be exercising (this could just be walking to and from school or walking the dog, or it could be a full-on sports match). Add that colour to the key.

7. Study time

Now you've marked off all the things you have to do in your week it's time to add in your study time. Study time is the time in which you do school work. This may be homework, coursework or revision.

A straight A student will use all the study time they have allocated themselves every week. If they've finished their most urgent homework and coursework, they will spend the remaining time on revision tasks; revision is not in addition to this study time, it is included.

These are the amounts of time I suggest you set aside for study. You might find that you need slightly more or slightly less depending on how efficiently you work and which subjects you're taking as some subjects can be more time-consuming than others.

Year 11 – 1 to 1.5 hours per week per subject. If you're doing 10 GCSEs that means you'll be doing 10 to 15 hours study at home per week.

Year 12 – 5 to 6 hours per week per subject. If you're doing 4 AS levels that means you'll be doing 20 to 24 hours study at home per week.

Year 13 – 6.5 to 7 hours per week per subject. If you're doing 3 A2's that means you'll be doing 19.5 to 21 hours study at home per week.

Your task is to slot this number of hours study into your weekly timetable. If you can't get this number of hours onto your weekly timetable because of all your other commitments you need to think about what you can give up in terms of interests, hobbies and part-time work. It's an important lesson to learn – you can't do everything! If you consciously decide to do less study time and more of other things then you should understand now that you're making a decision to get lower grades. It's your call.

Colour in the times when you'll be studying and add that colour to the key.

8. The time that's left...

Is there any time left over? Great! That time is yours. Use it as you wish – socialise, read, exercise, play music. Do what feels good to you and recharges you. But, most of all – enjoy!

9. Other?

You may find that there are other categories you want to add to your own weekly routine. I would encourage you to do this and to make this routine very much your own. So, if you want to add in specific slots for further reading, or colour code different out of school activities then please do this. Add as many categories to your routine as you need to make it meaningful and helpful to you.

A note about in-school study periods

When you're in Year 12 or 13 you will probably have timetabled study periods while you're in school.

If you want to minimise your stress and stay sane while you're studying for your A Levels you need to fully use this time. Some people like to allocate particular study periods to particular slots, e.g. you do chemistry homework on Monday period 4 or you do further reading (reading newspapers and periodicals) in the school library on Friday period 3. Otherwise, you could do your most urgent homework task in each study period. You need to discover what works for you but always use this time wisely and effectively.

What next?

Now you've created your weekly routine you need to start following it, and stick to it.

If it doesn't work for you, think about where it's failing. Is it your will-power that's failing, or is it something to do with the way your routine is organised? Re-jig your routine to suit your needs. Good routines aren't created over-night. You will need to have patience, testing it out to see what works for you and adjusting your routine accordingly.

A note about procrastination and getting started

I want you to remember this very important sentence:

Procrastination is a choice.

It is your choice how you spend your life. In every moment of every day you are actively choosing how you are spending your time. If you find yourself procrastinating you need to make a choice. Are you going to continue frittering away your time, or are you going to focus your energy on something that really matters to you; doing the work that will help you to achieve your hopes and dreams.

Sometimes procrastination can be a symptom of something else. As mentioned above, it can be because you haven't acknowledged your need for the time and space to transition from one activity to another. Alternatively, procrastination can occur when you have a task to do which you don't know how to do or don't know where to start. Look for the solution to this problem. It could be sitting down, breaking the task down into smaller, more achievable chunks and having a go. Or, you might need to seek help before you get started, in which case find another task to do that will help you move forward in another area.

If you're procrastinating because you feel discouraged by disappointing results for something have a conversation with yourself in your head telling yourself that the only way you're going to improve is by working at it (see step 2 on effort) and then set to applying yourself. Finally, you might find yourself procrastinating because you're tired. If this is the case make a decision: are you too tired to study? If yes, give yourself a break and work at another time. If no, get on with it and stop wasting time!

Your weekly routine

Time	Monday	Tuesday	Wednesday	Thursday	Friday	Saturday	Sunday
00:00							
01:00							
02:00							
03:00							
04:00							
05:00							
06:00							
07:00							
08:00							
09:00							
10:00							
11:00							
12:00							
13:00							
14:00							
15:00							
16:00							
17:00							
18:00							
19:00							
20:00							
21:00							
22:00							
23:00							

Key

Sleep		School		Study time		Meals	
Exercise		Hobbies /job		You-time		Self-care	

Chapter Summary

- Schedule your out of school time in the same way that you'd schedule your in-school time so that you know you're dedicating enough time each week to all the activities that are going to set you up for success in your exams.
- Allow time for everything from sleep to study and eating to exercise. If you follow your plan every week you'll arrive at exam time in peak condition in terms of your preparation and your physical and emotional readiness to do your best.
- If your schedule doesn't work for you perfectly in the first week then tweak it, change it and play with it until it does serve you.
- Procrastination is a choice. It's a symptom of an underlying problem. Diagnose the problem and solve it so that you can move on with your studies as planned.

Step 5
Get organised

This chapter includes:

- How to organise yourself to stay on top of your deadlines and keep yourself sane!

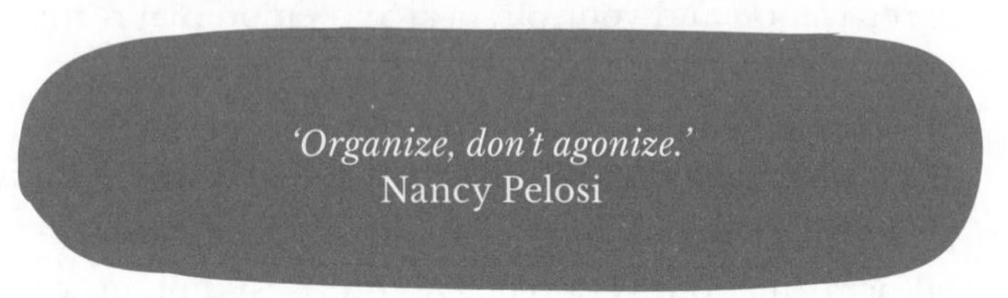

Once you've worked out how you're going to spend your time, you need to get yourself organised in other ways. You need to make sure that you have all the right equipment and tools to support you in getting the grades you want and you need to use them to their full benefit.

Your planner

The very first tool you need is a planning system. You can use an old-fashioned paper planner, either provided by your school or bought from a stationery shop, or you can use an electronic calendar or app. The purpose of your planner is to keep track of your to do list, deadlines and appointments. Whatever planning system you choose you need to make sure it's able to do these things.

The next step is to use your planner. Many students drift through a lot of school just using their memory to organise themselves. The more homework tasks you're set and the more deadlines you're given, the more important it gets to write it all down.

I was at school before smart phones or apps were even invented so I used a paper planner. When I was given a piece of homework,

I would write down what it was on the day in the planner when it was due in. I tended to complete tasks in the order in which they were due in with the most urgent first, followed by the second most urgent. However, if you have a very large project or piece of coursework to complete you need to plan that in over the days, weeks, or months leading up to the day when it is due in.

The best way to plan out a large task is to break it down into small sections and give each one of these small sections a 'due date'. This will enable you to complete the project or coursework on time without getting too stressed or having to stay up into the early hours of the morning to get it finished the day that it's due in.

As you complete each task that you've put in your planner you can cross it out, tick it off or delete it so that you know it's been done. Use the time you've set aside in your weekly routine to complete these tasks (see step 4).

Your filing system

You will really thank yourself in the long-term for keeping your lesson notes, homework tasks, worksheets, essays etc. neatly filed in a logical way. If you're working in exercise books then the key thing is to stick in worksheets and other resources in the order in which you used them. You also need to make sure that all tasks set are completed and in your book, this will mean you have a complete set of notes when it comes to revision time.

If you're using a paper-based system my suggestion is that you buy a lever arch file for each subject that you're studying and a set of dividers. Use the dividers to separate each topic or module that you study.

At the front of your lever arch file keep a copy of the topic list or exam specification for that subject. Then, in each divider section file all notes, worksheets, essays and resources in the chronological order of when that work was set.

You should also buy yourself a narrower A4 ring binder folder to carry around with you on a day-to-day basis. Again, put dividers in this folder separating out the different subjects that you're studying. Keep all your current notes and homework tasks in this folder and then, once per week, file these notes in your lever arch file at home. I think Friday afternoon, when you get home from school, is the perfect time for this. I call it 'Filing Friday'. While you're doing your weekly filing it's a good idea to check if your notes are complete from that week or if there's anything missing. Sometimes your teacher may not have found time to mark your work and hand it back to you. Other times you may have had to miss a lesson for some reason which means you have to catch-up with your class notes and homework.

You will also probably have files on the computer that you need to keep organised. I suggest that you use a hierarchical system where you have a folder for each subject, then folders for each topic or module inside each subject folder. Be vigilant about filing your digital files in the correct place at all times to keep your computer well organised.

Stationery and equipment

Having the right stationery or equipment with you for all your lessons is vital if you want to be able to focus on learning rather than fussing about asking the teacher for it, borrowing it from your friends or having to make do with tools that aren't up to the job. Students not having the right equipment is one of the biggest causes of time wasted in the classroom, particularly at A Level, so make sure you've got the right equipment to thrive.

The basics:

Have these with you every day (without fail!):

- A pen
- A pencil
- A ruler

The good-to-haves:

In addition to the basics you'll find your learning journey much smoother if you have the things listed below:

- Rubber
- Pencil sharpener
- Spare pen
- Spare pencil
- Maybe some coloured pens
- Colouring pencils
- If appropriate, mathematical equipment *e.g.* scientific calculator, set square, protractor, compass (you'll need these for maths and other subjects where you draw graphs like science and geography).
- A pencil case to keep it all in
- Highlighters

Paper:
You'll also need something to write on!

- Lined paper – everyone will need this
- Plain paper – I think it's an excellent idea to have some of this e.g. for drawing diagrams, mind-maps, maps, field drawings, sketches etc.
- Graph paper – depending on what subjects you're taking
- You might also like to invest in A3 paper (for making revision posters or larger diagrams) and note cards, also known as index cards, (for making revision flash cards).

Go to lifemoreextraordinary.com/workbook to get a complete stationery shopping list for the beginning of the school year to make sure you've got everything you need to stay organised and succeed in your studies.

Chapter Summary

- Staying organised is really important so that you don't fall behind with your deadlines, you minimise your stress and you are always in the position to complete classwork and homework tasks to the best of your ability.
- A planner is vital to keep track of deadlines, your timetable and appointments.
- Having the right stationery and keeping on top of your filing will ensure that you have all the notes ready when you want to start revision. Make a regular appointment with yourself for your own 'Filing Friday'.
- Making sure you've got the right stationery and equipment with you at every lesson will lead to a slicker learning experience.

Step 6
Study Habits For Success

This chapter includes:

- How good study habits help you to achieve your dreams
- What are mini-habits and how to incorporate them into your life
- How to choose and maintain good habits

> *'It's not what we do once in a while that shapes our lives. It's what we do consistently.'*
> Anthony Robbins

When you're working towards getting amazing exam grades, you need to build habits that support your dreams. Habits are actions that we take consistently, everyday (or even more often), as a matter of course, without even really thinking about it. You've already got hundreds of habits from reflexively checking your phone for new notifications to turning onto your left side after you turn the light out to go to sleep. These habits have developed unconsciously over months and years. However, when you're thinking about good study habits that support you in achieving your dreams you need to make some very conscious decisions about which habits you want to adopt and where they will fit into your life.

Your weekly routine that you created in Step 4 and the things you did to organise yourself in Step 5 provide the foundation for your successful habits. However, there are lots of smaller habits that you can incorporate into this structure that will see you making consistently faster progress towards your goals.

'When you start taking consistent action, you will see results.'
Marie Forleo

Stephen Guise wrote a book called *Mini Habits: Smaller Habits, Bigger Results* which talks about how he used habits, which on the surface appear to be ridiculously small actions, to radically improve his fitness and write a book, amongst other things. When you incorporate the idea of mini-habits into your study routine they can be just as transformational.

After repeatedly failing to go to the gym for a full workout, Stephen discovered that if he gave himself a stupidly small goal it was much easier to get started. And, once he got started, he more often than not exceeded his goal. The stupidly small goal that he gave himself was to do one push-up every day. What he found was that it was easy to achieve this habit and he'd often find that while he was doing his one push up he'd do a few more.

Stephen turned his mini-habit of one daily push-up into an exercise regime where he now goes to the gym several times a week. The point was that he started so small it was impossible to fail.

People come to me on a regular basis asking for advice about getting motivated to revise, how to revise, how to study and all sorts of other topics related to their academic success. Underlying most of their questions and concerns is a real worry that the task is simply too big; they will never be able to learn their course content in time for the exam or sit down for three hours every evening to do their homework.

If your study tasks are too large then I suggest you reduce them down to mini-habits and see how you get on. In this step, I'm going to suggest some really powerful mini study habits to you and show you how you can turn them into proper habits that you do automatically every day.

To give you an idea of how powerful these habits can be I want to tell you about one of my readers. Sophie wrote to me after she got her GCSE results to tell me how helpful she'd found the idea of mini-habits, which I originally shared in a blog post. Sophie told me that she'd achieved 11 A*s and an A and said this about mini-habits:

> *'One of the most effective blog posts for me was the one on the mini study habits. I especially found the 5-minute revision session really worthwhile and also reading through class notes at the end of the day. I found they're both actually really easy habits to add into your after school routine so they'll definitely be ones I'll try to stick to! Thank you so much for the ideas which I really think did help to boost my grades that little bit more.'*

7 Powerful Mini-Habits

Do five minutes of revision every day

Imagine the effect on your grades if you revised for 5 minutes per day every day. That would mean revising for 35 minutes per week or 150 minutes per month (2.5 hours). This is approximately 20 hours if you did five minutes of revision every day between the beginning of the school year and the end of April, roughly when exam season begins.

The impact of adding a measly five minutes of revision to your daily life between now and your exams would be huge. There would be so much that you had committed to memory before you even started thinking seriously about revision. How much easier would that make your life in exam season? How much would it improve your grades by?

The benefits of doing five minutes of revision every day from the start of the school year include:

- Helping you learn the course content months ahead of exam season
- Getting you to experiment with revision techniques so you find out what works for you

- Creating a revision habit that will serve you well as you approach your exams

So, what should you be revising in your daily five minute revision session?

- Memorise quotes from texts for English Literature
- Memorise dates for history
- Practice spellings of complicated technical words for the sciences and geography
- Practice drawing diagrams of scientific processes
- Memorise definitions of subject vocabulary
- Learn vocabulary or verbs for foreign languages
- Look at a historical source (picture or short text) and brainstorm what you can see
- Pick a theme from a text for English and write down as many examples of it as you can think of from the text
- Act out a story, scientific process or historical or political event
- Solve a maths problem
- Memorise a formula
- Memorise key facts for a case study

I will give you much more detail about how to actually revise in the revision section of the book (steps 8 and 9) but this gives you some ideas on where to get started with your daily revision habit.

Read through a page of class notes at the end of each day

A friend of mine at Cambridge University did this every day after lectures and it served her very well; I wish I'd done it at the time. It's the very first step in your revision process and will:

- Start fixing your class learning in your mind
- Show you if there's anything you don't fully understand
- Show you where you might have gaps in your work

You can then take steps, such as asking your teacher to go through something you don't understand in more detail with you, to get a full understanding or fill in the gaps. This means you won't be scrabbling around in exam season trying to understand things for the first time. Instead, you'll be able to focus on learning it and practicing your exam technique.

Write down your homework at the end of each lesson

In step 5, we talked about the importance of having a planner. If you have trouble disciplining yourself to use it, then this is an excellent mini-habit for you to adopt. It's the most important first step you can take towards getting your target grades, staying organised and meeting your deadlines. It's fundamental to getting good grades. If you're not already doing this, don't skip it!

Self-monitor your learning

When you're revising, taking notes, reading, watching an educational video or doing any other study task you should always be asking yourself 'is this learning experience working for me?' This is essential if you're going to learn successfully and efficiently. There is no point in carrying on revising in a certain way if it doesn't help you to remember. There is no point in carrying on reading a text if your brain is too tired and needs a ten minute break.

Aim to ask yourself: 'Is this learning experience working for me?' once per day and adjust yourself according to the answer. If you ask yourself the question more often your learning will be even more focused, efficient and successful as a result.

File notes in the right place every day

Wondering around with a folder full of crumpled and disordered notes? This isn't going to help you meet deadlines or keep track of what you've already learned. When you come to creating revision materials and notes you will thank yourself for keeping everything organised.

At the minimum, make sure you file lesson notes in a divider for each subject, and in date order, in the file that you carry around with you every day. Once a week take the time to file them into your subject file at home (Filing Friday!).

Read one online article everyday

Extra reading really helps to cement ideas that you've learned in class and place them in a wider context. It's also really important for university applications. Create a habit of reading one online article related to one of your subjects every single day.

There's more about reading around your subject in Step 7.

Review your day

At the end of each day ask yourself these three questions:

1. What went well?
2. What didn't go well?
3. How could you improve?

This kind of self-reflection helps you move forward and constantly do better.

Choose a maximum of three mini-habits

You may be feeling a little bit smug because you already do several (or all) of the study mini-habits I've suggested. That's great! However, if you're not doing most of them you need to choose three.

In the workbook (www.lifemoreextraordinary.com/workbook) write down which three you think you are most likely to succeed with. Don't try and do too many at once as you're more likely to fail!

Complete your mini-habits every day.

One of the essential features of mini-habits is that they happen every day; you never get a day off. The habit is so small that it can be done whatever else is going on that day.

By completing the habit every day you are training yourself to make the habit stick and you are reducing the amount of willpower it will take to complete the habit. The problem with having a day off from a habit is that it's too easy to have another day off and another day off. There's a huge power in making it non-negotiable.

Some days you can exceed your mini-habit. For example, you might read two articles about subjects you're studying at school. You might read ten. But, you're successful if you meet your minimum requirement (and that's all you should do on Christmas Day or your birthday!).

Track your mini-habits

Print off a calendar so you can track your mini-habits. (You can get a mini-habits tracking calendar from www.lifemoreextraordinary.com/workbook). Everyday tick off when you've completed all the mini-habits you've set yourself. Day-by-day, when you tick to show you've completed your mini-habits, you'll see the progress you're making towards your dream grades. This will inspire you to keep going.

How to create better study habits that work for you

Now we've identified some mini study habits to get you started, let's talk about how you start good habits and keep them going in more detail. I found the book *Better Than Before: Mastering the Habits of Our Everyday Lives* by Gretchen Rubin really informative in learning more about habit formation, and the ideas in the rest of this step are inspired by Rubin's book.

Know your habits personality

The first step is to know your habits personality type. In her book, Gretchen Rubin identifies four habit personality types:

- **Upholders** who like to meet their own expectations of themselves as well as everyone else's expectations for them.
- **Questioners** who question all expectations, and they respond to an expectation only if they conclude that it makes sense.
- **Obligers** who like to please everyone around them but don't do anything to meet their own expectations for themselves
- **Rebels** resist all expectations, both of themselves and from other people.

Which do you think you are? I'm an upholder and I strongly suspect that this tendency played a large part in me getting five A Grades at A Level: I had strong expectations of myself and made myself publicly accountable by saying what I was aiming for. Luckily, Rubin has created a little quiz on her website where you can find out your habits personality. You're welcome to go and take Rubin's test - there's a link to the quiz in the workbook www.lifemoreextraordinary.com/workbook.

Now, let's talk about how to start and maintain good study habits.

Begin

The first thing you've got to do if you want to up your study habit is begin. You can either do this small by creating a mini study habit or you can have a 'blast start' (Rubin's words) where you go all in with a full-blown study routine, this is like the one I showed you how to plan in step 4.

The key is to start, and start now. I've already used this quote from William Wordsworth but it's so true in its simplicity that I'm using it again: '*To begin, begin*'.

Wipe the slate clean

The best time to start something beneficial to you is now, but sometimes it's easier to start when you've got a clean slate. So, at the beginning of a new school year, after a half-term holiday or when you change schools; it's like drawing a line under what you were like before and saying: 'This is the new me, and this is how the new me behaves.'

As Rubin says, always make sure you follow your desired habits on a Monday. If you don't you'll be tempted to ignore them for the rest of the week.

Get struck by lightning

No, I don't mean go and stand out in a thunderstorm and wait until you get struck by lightning; that would be outright stupid. What I mean, or what Rubin meant when she wrote about it in her book, was to use a moment of profound change or realisation to change your habits.

Maybe you've really been meaning to change your habits but can't quite bring yourself to. You keep getting mainly B's with a few C's and the odd A. Then one day you get a D, or an E.

In that moment you know something has to change. You've been watching your habits slipping for a while but, in this moment, you see things clearly. Things are changing now and there is no looking back.

Create your schedule

In step 4, I showed you how to create yourself a weekly schedule so if you didn't actually do it straight after you'd read that chapter, I want you to go and do it now. To be successful with your grades, and build that success consistently over a whole school year, you need to create yourself a study schedule which you stick to. The secret to this strategy's success is that it ensures that you're consistent in applying yourself to your studies week-by-week and month-by-month over the whole school year.

> *'Every great accomplishment rests on the foundation of what came before it.'*
> Stephen Guise

Creating a schedule and sticking to it is easier if you're an upholder like me and you work well with being accountable to yourself. If you're a questioner you justify it by saying 'I need to apply myself consistently if I'm going to get the grades that I really want and achieve my dream'. If you're an obliger you make yourself accountable to someone else. If you're a rebel, well, I don't really know how to help you, you're a law unto yourself!

Build your solid foundation

In step 3, we talked about how important it was to look after yourself: get enough sleep, eat well, exercise and have some time for yourself to do whatever you like. When you created your weekly routine in Chapter 4 you should have prioritised these things. When eating well, exercising and a regular bedtime are programmed into your routine it is much easier to maintain these good habits. If you stick to your routine, you'll stick to your habits. Simple. Don't let late nights, a Big Mac® or the lure of the TV remote and the sofa distract you from maintaining your strong foundation.

Keep yourself accountable

Making yourself accountable to someone else is a proven way to maintain good habits, particularly if you're an obliger.

You might well use accountability already in your daily life without knowing it. You turn up to school on time because the daily register holds you accountable. You get to Sainsbury's on time for your shift on the tills because you'd get fired if you didn't. You feed your dog when you get in from school because of the beseeching look in his marmalade eyes as he sits over his food bowl.

The thing here is to make yourself accountable for your study habits to someone else. You get to choose. Accountability is one of the key things that I offer to my long term clients, really helping them to form and stick to good study habits. However, you could report into your mum or dad, a sibling, a friend or anyone else to keep you accountable. This could take the form of texting or telling them when you're starting your study time and when you finish. Alternatively, you might like to have a 'study date' with a friend where you get together and study because that's what you're there to do. Or, you could have a weekly meeting with me to check in on your progress and assess how well you're sticking to your targets.

Monitor your progress

Keeping track of whether you're consistently sticking to your plans is really important in maintaining good habits. If you've ever got 100% attendance you'll know the satisfaction that brings.

Printing off a calendar and ticking off when you stick to your habit every day can give you enormous satisfaction. I used to do this with my revision plan; every time I'd revised a topic on the plan I ticked it off. With my weekly routine I held myself mentally accountable (I could do this because I was an upholder and find it relatively easy to hold myself to promises I've made to myself).

If you're struggling to maintain a study habit, start ticking off every day that you've stuck with it so that you feel that sense of building accomplishment every day. Remember, you can get a habits tracking calendar from www.lifemoreextraordinary.com/workbook.

Give it up

If there's something that is really distracting you from your studies then a simple solution can be to give it up. I used to be an Australian soap opera addict. Everyday I'd waste an hour of my life watching *Neighbours* and *Home and Away.* About halfway through Year 11, I realised that I had to use that time more productively if I wanted to get the grades I needed to achieve my dream of going to Cambridge.

I gave up watching both my Aussie soaps then and there and spent that time studying. For me it's easier to say an outright no to some things than to say, 'everything in moderation'. That's what enabled me to give up chocolate for 15 months once and I've now gone two years without caffeine. If I have a little then I want a lot, that's why I need to give up.

If there's something that you know you can't do in moderation, just say no!

Make it easy for yourself

You're more likely to follow some habits if you make them convenient, or easy, to follow. So, if you're trying to develop the habit of five minutes of revision every day then you'll make it easier for yourself if you carry your revision cards with you wherever you go. Then you can revise whenever you get a minute.

On a grander scale, you might make home study more convenient by having a nice desk with a comfy chair, lots of nice stationery and some peaceful music in the background.

Make it hard for yourself

Conversely, if there are things that make it hard for you to follow your desired study habit make them harder to do. If you can't help checking your phone for *Facebook* notifications every five minutes while you're supposed to be doing homework, leave it outside the room, or at least on the other side of the room. Even better, turn all the notifications off, or delete the app!

On Christmas Eve 2014, I deleted the *Facebook* app from my phone. *Facebook* was becoming a real problem in my life; I was constantly reading and checking it and really annoying my children, my husband and all the rest of my friends and family. I told myself I would only delete it for four days (over the Christmas period) but I've never put it back on. I can still check *Facebook* on my iPad or laptop, I'm not missing out. I'm just looking at it when I've got time and not when I'm with other people who want and deserve my attention.

The question I'd like you to ask yourself here is: what's more important to me? Five minutes on *Snapchat* or working towards my dream? You have to balance the easy option in the here and now with your dream for your future.

Stop the excuses

You know last week when you stopped studying to catch *EastEnders* twice, despite your study schedule saying that you no longer watch *EastEnders* at that time? You told yourself you'd go back to your studies afterwards but you got sucked in by the telly and never went back.

If you hadn't given yourself the chance to watch *EastEnders* you'd have stayed studying for at least an hour longer. You were telling yourself that you deserved a break. Actually, you were weakening your study habit and your grades, in the process. Don't make these kind of lame excuses. Stick with the plan. If you can't stand to miss *EastEnders* then record it and watch it on catch-up when you've done your studies for the day.

Prevent self-sabotage

Have you ever promised yourself that you'll start eating healthily only to be offered a cake for someone's birthday at break time? You know you shouldn't but you cave straight away because, 'it would be rude not to'.

The same kind of sabotage can happen with your study intentions. You've promised yourself you're going to go to that quiet corner in the library in your free period. But at break time your friend says they're going to pop into town and would you like to join them?

It sounds so much more fun that burying your head in your biology text book and learning about excretion for an hour. So you say yes. The problem is you've just sabotaged your good study habit.

The way to deal with this is to make a plan in your head for offers like this so that you anticipate things that might throw you off course. You could just plan out that you'll say to your friend 'sorry, but I'm going to the library to get my biology homework done.' Don't say 'maybe next time'.

Think of all the ways that your good intentions regularly get sabotaged and come up with a plan for how you're going to prevent that sabotage. Then you'll be ready next time someone throws you off course.

Know yourself

In her book, Rubin covered many more strategies to create good habits. It's an entertaining and insightful read that I'd highly recommend.

The strongest message that came out of her book for me was that you should know yourself and work with yourself to improve your habits. So, if you know that sitting down to enjoy an episode of *EastEnders* is a real treat for you and helps you get through your day, build it into your routine, but don't let one episode of *EastEnders* turn into aimless TV watching for hours on end.

Always be mindful of your own behaviours and natural reactions. If you spot dangerous habits emerging then come up with strategies that will turn them into good habits that will serve your goals.

Your plan for good study habits

Answer the questions below to start building your plan for good study habits. All the questions are in the workbook with plenty of space for you to write your answers down: www.lifemoreextraordinary.com/workbook.

1. Which three study habits are you doing to start adding into your routine today?
2. Use the table below to identify the things that most often pull you away from your good intentions and good habits. What steps can you take to stay on track and stay focused on the things that are going to help you to achieve your hopes and dreams?

Good Study Habit	What stops you?	How can you make it happen in the future?

Chapter Summary

1. Good study habits will support you in your desire to get the grades that will help you access your dream.
2. Mini-habits are a great place to start. Choose up to three good study habits that are so stupidly small that you can't help but do them every single day.
3. Knowing your habits personality will help you to start and stick to any new habits that you adopt - knowing yourself is the first step to successful habit formation.
4. Creating a schedule, tracking your good habits and having an accountability buddy are great ways to keep yourself on track with your good habits and good intentions.

PART III
Fall in Love with Your Studies

Learning is at its most powerful when you take control of the process. If you take a personal interest in what you're being taught in the classroom and take your interest beyond the school setting then you will not only become a truly excellent student but also fall in love with your studies.

The students who I work with who have done this are the ones who stand a very strong chance of being accepted into elite universities like Oxford and Cambridge. They're also the people who are sufficiently resourceful to be irresistible to future employers. This step is essential if you want to achieve true academic excellence.

Step 7
Widen your knowledge

'An investment in knowledge pays the best interest.'
Benjamin Franklin

This chapter includes:

- How to move from being a student to an enthusiast
- How to make what you learn in the classroom seem like the basics
- How to impress your teachers and, more importantly, your examiners with your broad and wide-ranging knowledge of your subjects
- How to give yourself an extra boost when you start thinking about the next stage of life *e.g.* applying for university or getting a job

One of the best things you can do to take command of a subject is to widen your knowledge. What I mean is, don't just learn what is taught to you in the classroom by memory. Take ownership of the subject and become an enthusiast for it. You will become genuinely curious and interested in it and start to seek information beyond what is taught to you in the classroom.

'Any fool can know. The point is to understand.'
Albert Einstein

How will broadening my knowledge help me in my exams?

When you broaden your knowledge of a subject, you go beyond the basics. You move from just knowing facts, to a deeper level of understanding. For example, if you're studying a book such as 'Pride and Prejudice' it's very easy just to read it as a gripping story that you just can't put down. However, you can also view a classic such as this as social commentary of the time. In order to do this, you might read a biography of the author Jane Austen. You could also read another one of her novels and try to learn a little bit about contemporary events; the social, economic and political background of it all, or read a book of literary criticism on Pride and Prejudice.

When you take these steps you will start to see things like:

- Patterns in the way the author structures books and uses language
- The extent to which the book is a product of the time, or an exception for when it was written
- How the book reflects the people, politics and society of its day.

You may not directly write about any of these things in an essay, but all of it will help to add nuance, colour and depth to what you say. It will also help you to start thinking about your own writing, how you structure your essays and how you use language to explain your points.

Broadening your knowledge isn't confined to English literature. If you're studying biology, you might make a point of recording and watching any documentaries on TV about genetics. If you're studying history you might watch history documentaries or go to a site of historical interest, like the Tower of London or Stonehenge. If maths is your thing you might like to get to grips with some computer programming languages or read about Alan Turing and the work he did at Bletchley Park. There really is no end to the ways you can broaden your learning, it's just important to do it. As you broaden your knowledge, you set what you learn in the classroom in context, learn more about each subject as a whole and become more passionate and enthusiastic so that you just want to learn more and more.

How to widen your knowledge

I've collected a list of ideas here for how you can broaden your knowledge of your subject. It's not all reading; there are lots of things you can do other than sitting in a chair with a book. However, this list isn't exhaustive. You may well come up with other things that you can do for your subjects that will help you widen your knowledge and become an enthusiast for each subject that you're studying. It would be a really good idea to talk to your subject teachers to see what they'd recommend you do on a daily basis e.g. which newspapers, magazines, periodicals or websites you should regularly read, as well as any recommendations for days out or whole books you could read that would support each topic that you study.

It's an excellent idea as well to keep a record of your further reading. I recommend to my clients that they keep a notebook where they write down the titles of the books they read as well as a brief summary of what the book was about and any thoughts that arise while they're reading it or questions that are raised in their minds. You might also like to jot down interesting quotes. You can either do this in a paper notebook or use a notes app like Evernote so that you've always got it with you.

For interesting articles that you find you could cut them out of newspapers, photocopy them or print them off. Keep a special section in your lever arch file for further reading articles that are particularly interesting or relevant to your studies so that you can easily refer back to them.

You could also use an app like Pinterest or Pocket to save articles. Setting up shared Pinterest boards with people in your class to share articles that you find is a great idea as you'll be helping each other. If you prefer to keep your reading more private you can use an app like Pocket or even save articles to Evernote.

Finally, a great place to find relevant articles for your subjects is on Twitter. There are hundreds of teachers on Twitter tweeting out relevant articles to their students. Many of these teachers join together in subject groups using subject specific hashtags to share articles with their students and between schools. This is a very rich resource and the teachers are doing all the hard work for you; I'd strongly recommend that you start using it, even if your teachers are not actively tweeting.

Go to www.lifemoreextraordinary.com/workbook to get a link to the best subject specific hashtags and accounts to follow on twitter.

25 ideas for widening your knowledge

- Read novels by the same authors that you're studying.
- Read biographies and autobiographies of novelists, poets, famous scientists, historical figures, politicians, kings and queens.
- Read the newspaper, new scientific research, reviews of plays, political insight and economic analysis. Find a couple of articles per day that are relevant to what you're studying and read them. Cut them out if they're directly relevant to your course and file them.
- Follow blogs and online news sites, maybe you've got a favourite scientist who is also a blogger or big on social media and make a point of reading their posts.
- Read online news sites – see how the same story is written up on sites with different political points of view. Which view do you have most sympathy with? If you find a particularly helpful or relevant article for your course, bookmark it or print it out and add it to your notes for future reference.
- Create a Pinterest board for each subject you study, or even for each module, and follow other pinners who have similar interests. You could even set up Pinterest group boards with other people in your class for each subject to share resources that you find.
- Watch travel shows on the TV, there are some great travel shows that take you to unexplored areas of the earth

throwing up issues to do with social justice, global warming, economic disparities etc. They're great entertainment, they expand your horizons and give you a new perspective on what you're studying.

- Listen to radio shows and podcasts. I love Radio 4 and there are some wonderful programmes on there. If you're a numbers person, tune into *More or Less*, and if you're a feminist then *Woman's Hour* might be your thing. Studying psychology? *All in the Mind*. There's a Radio 4 show for just about every academic subject. Find out what it is and either make a point of listening live, or to the podcast.
- Watch films. Biopics have been made about many historic and important people; they're an easy and enjoyable way to use up two hours of leisure time, enjoying yourself and feeling like you're improving yourself at the same time. If you're studying a Shakespeare play you could find a film of it, or even two, watch them and compare the presentation of the script. If you're studying a particular period of history there's probably a film set at that time; it will give you a taste of the way people lived, the clothes they wore and the way they thought.
- Go to an historical re-enactment.
- Go on a field trip.
- Go to the theatre and watch anything, whether you're studying it specifically or not. It will really enrich your mind. When I was doing A Level English, my mum took me to the National Theatre in London to see Othello and it was absolutely amazing; the vision of it sticks in my mind to this day. It was far more memorable than sitting at an uncomfortable desk in a class full of girls, all of us taking the various parts in the play.
- Go to museums. Find one near you that covers your subject or make a special trip to go somewhere further afield; many museums in the UK now have free entry.
- Go to an art gallery. The National Portrait Gallery would be a useful place to go if you're studying history to look at how important people of their day were portrayed. The

National Gallery will give you an insight into the culture of the time, by what was viewed as important enough to represent in art. There will also be art galleries near to where you live. Find out where they are and take a trip one Saturday afternoon.

- Attend conferences, symposiums, lectures and conventions on your subject. This is a great way to immerse yourself in a subject and meet some of the most prominent contemporary thinkers in your field. Make these big minds and their ideas really come alive by coming into direct contact with them.
- Go to a festival. Book, music, art and poetry festivals are common around the country all year round.
- Go on a long walk to look at landforms you've been studying in geography or geology.
- Go to political meetings.
- Join a campaigning group on a subject you care about e.g. Amnesty International on Human Rights or Greenpeace on Global Warming.
- Join an archaeological dig.
- Go to a place that has been used as a case study in the classroom.
- Get a job or become a volunteer working at a local historic house or museum.
- Volunteer on a conservation project.
- Get work experience in a related career e.g. journalism or publishing for English, in a business that interests you for business studies, in a constituency office for politics, in a local laboratory for science.
- Subscribe to a relevant magazine e.g. New Scientist, National Geographic, The Economist, The New Statesman - anything that helps you to learn about your subject in a broader or deeper way.

You by no means have to do all of the things listed here. Choose the ones that appeal most to you. If you don't much like reading but love a good movie, find some that are relevant to what you're studying. If you find it hard to find time for day trips because of your other commitments make a point of going to one place of interest connected to your studies while you're on holiday and focus on further reading the rest of the time.

The thing that will make you most successful in widening your knowledge is consistency. In step 4, I mentioned how I used to read the newspaper every day when I came home from school. I used to make a point of looking at the science pages as I was studying both biology and chemistry. Nowadays, having a daily newspaper is pretty rare, so find an alternative. Reading the science section of the BBC news website would be an excellent alternative to reading the newspaper. Also, check the TV listings regularly to see if there's a programme that's interesting to you and record it so you can watch it when you've got time.

The key to success here is to turn these things into habits like we previously talked about in step 6. If you read one relevant article every day while you're studying for your A Levels, over a two year period you will build up a huge stock of relevant knowledge that will really flesh out and add detail to your understanding of your subject. Reading alternative points of view and ways of explaining knowledge other than what is presented in your course textbook will also widen your perspective and give you the chance to develop your intellectual flexibility. You will no longer be a student, you will be a knowledgeable enthusiast with enormous confidence in your command of your subject come the time of your exam.

'It is the absence of facts that frightens people: the gap you open, into which they pour their fears, fantasies, desires.'
Wolf Hall, Hilary Mantel

Your plan to widen your knowledge

Use the questions below to make a plan for how you're going to widen your knowledge. Go to www.lifemoreextraordinary.com/workbook and download the workbook so that you can write your answers down.

1. Which of the 25 ideas listed above appeal to you most? List five ideas below.
2. Which ideas will you start with? Where are you going to find the books, articles, films or resources that you need?
3. Add a regular time slot into the weekly routine that you created in step 4 for widening your knowledge. This could be 20 minutes per day or an hour on a Sunday morning. You choose what works best for you and make it work for yourself.

Chapter Summary

- You are more likely to fall in love with any subject that you're studying if you make the effort to learn more about it than what is taught in the classroom.
- You will put your classroom learning into context when you go to the effort to learn more and your learning will become entrenched, deep learning, rather than information that's merely held in your short-term memory.
- Choose how you're going to go about widening your knowledge; choose the methods that excite you the most.
- Keep records of what you've done so that when you come to apply to university it's easy for you to write your personal statement.

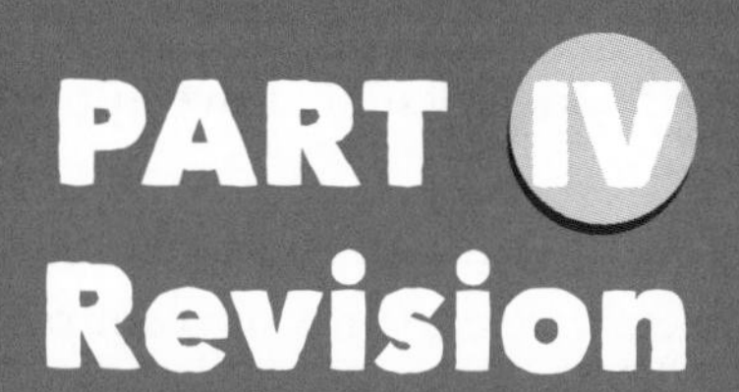

As you move through the school year, getting closer and closer to exam season, your teachers, peers and parents will start to talk to you about revision.

What is revision?

The *Pocket Oxford Dictionary* states that 'revision' is a word with Latin roots that means 'see (or read) again'.

This implies that in order to revise you have to have already learned what you're trying to revise. It isn't revision until you've done that.

The purpose of revision is two-fold:

1. To be able to remember all the knowledge you need for your exams.
2. To practice all the skills you need for your exams until you're perfect. For example, your exam technique (how to answer the questions in your exam to get the maximum number of marks).

To be revision ready in exam season, you need to have put the work in earlier in the year. That's what the previous seven chapters have been all about but don't worry, if you haven't been doing these things throughout the school year all is not lost. You'll just have to work a little bit harder when you get to exam season.

In the following two chapters, I'm going to explain to you firstly how to plan your revision so that you make it really effective. Secondly, I'll show you how to actually revise so that you are as efficient and effective as possible with your studies.

Step 8
Planning your revision

This chapter includes:

- Know what it takes to pass this exam
- How to identify which skills and areas of knowledge you need to focus on
- How to decide which revision techniques you should be using
- How to create a revision timetable

> *"One important key to success is self-confidence.*
> *An important key to self-confidence is preparation."*
> Arthur Ashe

Know what it takes to pass this exam

Here's one comforting piece of wisdom: there is no exam that will examine you on everything. It's not possible. Not everything is yet known. The scope of what will be tested in any exam is limited and this is a great thing. What you need to do, in order to ace your exam, is find out what the exam can cover. For school level exams this will be listed out in a document called the 'syllabus' or the 'specification'. The terms syllabus and specification are pretty much used interchangeably.

I'm going to explain to you here how to get a definitive breakdown of the knowledge and skills you need to pass a school-level exam, so that you can methodically ensure you have ticked everything off the list, and walk into the exam hall bursting with confidence.

Luckily for you the vast majority of school-level exam syllabuses have been through a pretty rigorous process of approval before they start being taught in schools. This means that what is required of you, the student, is generally quite reasonable in terms of the knowledge and skills you need to master. Use the page of the workbook provided at www.lifemoreextraordinary.com/workbook to collect together the names of all the exam boards and specifications that you're following and keep it all nicely organised. Here are the steps you need to take to make sure you're doing everything to meet the demands of the syllabus.

1. Find out what syllabus you are following. To do this, you need to ask your teacher which exam board and specification they are using.
2. Get access to a copy of the syllabus. Some teachers will have given you a copy of the syllabus at some point during the course, or they may have given you a simplified version of the syllabus. If they have given you a simplified version, or they haven't given you a copy at all, you need to use the powers of the internet to get your own copy of the original syllabus. (When you go to www.lifemoreextraordinary.com/workbook you'll see a link to a blog post where I've created a video to show you how to find your exam specifications online if you're not sure how to go about it).
3. While you're getting a copy of the syllabus, make sure you have information about both the knowledge you need to have as well as the skills you need to display in the exam. For example, you might have to have essay writing skills, or the ability to manipulate formulae, or use statistical techniques to analyse data. The content of your course, in terms of both skills and knowledge will be explained in the syllabus. Print off the bits that show the course content - don't print off the whole lot as there's usually dozens of pages that aren't particularly useful to you as a student.
4. Get hold of some past exam papers and mark schemes. Good teachers will drill their students for exams with multiple past-papers and share the mark schemes with their pupils. If this hasn't been your experience, you should be able to access lots of past papers or example papers, and their mark

schemes, on the exam board's website. The video I directed you to earlier shows you how to find these too.

Once you have the lists of content for all the subjects that you're taking you've got a list to work from. If you know everything on that list by the time you take the exam you'll have set yourself up very well to get an amazing grade.

Identify your strengths and weaknesses

> *'My weaknesses... I wish I could come up with something. I'd probably have the same pause if you asked me what my strengths are. Maybe they're the same thing.'*
> Al Pacino

By the end of this step, you're going to be two steps ahead of Al Pacino. You will know what your strengths and your weaknesses are as far as your exam syllabus is concerned.

First, though, I'm going to tell you a little story from my own experience.

When I was studying GCSE science, as we went through the course we had module tests that counted towards our final mark, as well as final exams which made up the majority of our marks. I was pretty good at science but there was one module I really struggled with. It was electricity and magnetism. One of the big problems was that we were being taught this topic by a newly qualified teacher, who was a biology specialist. Her way of teaching this topic was to copy the contents of the textbook onto the blackboard (yes, I'm that old) and have us copy that into our exercise books. She didn't explain anything and didn't do many experiments with us. Unsurprisingly, we didn't really learn anything, let alone understand it.

When it came to the module exam I achieved a pretty rotten result. I was gutted, but I knew what the problem was and I was determined to solve it. I wanted to get an A* for my science GCSE and I couldn't let bad teaching get in my way.

I went to my local library and borrowed another text book that was specifically about electricity and magnetism. I read and re-read this book, taking notes and reading it out loud until I had a solid grasp of this subject. To this day, I still wouldn't profess to have a really deep understanding of it, but I managed to do enough to prevent electricity and magnetism from being such a big gap in my knowledge that I couldn't get my A*. I'm happy to say that on results day I had achieved my aim and was awarded a double A* for my double GCSE in science.

What can you learn from my experience?

> *"I am always doing that which I cannot do, in order that I may learn how to do it."*
> Pablo Picasso

What I did in the example above was to identify one of my prime areas of weakness, based on the content of the course, and to take steps to tackle it. When you're taking an exam, you cannot ignore your areas of weakness as you can be asked anything on the syllabus. There will always be things that you're naturally better at and would prefer to come up in the exam, but you can't leave your grades to chance.

You may not have had the experience that one section of the course was particularly badly taught, you may just find one section is harder, or maybe when it was being covered in class you had some time off sick or you were distracted by something else going on in your life. Now is the time to identify these areas and make a plan to tackle them.

How to identify your strengths and weaknesses

Most of the time you will have a gut feel about which things you find easy and which things you find difficult. Use this method to mark your strengths and weaknesses onto your specifications:

1. Get some red, orange and green pens or highlighters.
2. On your syllabus, textbook contents page or checklist of what you need to know given to you by school, mark each topic area like so:
    a. Red – you don't understand it or can't remember it at all
    b. Orange – you're OK with it but not entirely confident
    c. Green – you understand it and can remember it really well

If you're not sure about how you feel about a topic, go back to your notes on that area and have a look at your assessed work. See what marks you were awarded for work you handed in. Were the marks equal to your target grade, or below? If they were below, mark them as red, if they were above put them as green and if they were equal to your target grades mark them as orange.

When you're planning out your revision your priority should be to start by revising the things you marked in red: your weaknesses. When you've finished those move on to the orange things and then, finally, the things you marked in green. By doing this you will be focusing on your areas of weakness, the parts of the syllabus where you are most likely to lose marks in your exam. As you go through your revision, you'll probably find that your areas of weakness change. Because you're focusing attention on certain areas they will turn into strengths and you will have to re-evaluate your strengths and weaknesses as you go along.

Seek help where you need it

Once you get into revision season time really is of the essence. This means that if you're really, really struggling with something you need to seek help rather than work it out on your own. Find a time to talk to a teacher or lecturer about your areas of difficulty, and move onto something you can progress on your own.

> *'Build up your weaknesses until they become your strong points.'*
> Knute Rockne

Which revision techniques should you be using?

Now you know which subject content you need to prioritise in your revision, you need to know how you should be revising.

Everyone has slightly different ways of learning. I know that I learn best by reading, talking to other people about ideas and discussing things. Other people will learn best by doing – whether this is experimenting with things, making things or acting them out. In order to revise successfully you need to have a strong understanding of how *you* learn. Without this understanding you could waste an awful lot of time sitting at a desk achieving very little.

Learning styles

There has been a lot of research done into different learning styles. One of the most popular classifications of learning styles is visual, auditory and kinaesthetic.

- Visual – seeing or reading
- Auditory – listening or talking
- Kinaesthetic – touching and doing

You will probably have heard these terms used before. These are not the only learning styles that have been identified but they're a useful starting point. However, everyone is different. Everyone has a different balance of the learning styles.

What is most valuable to you is understanding what kinds of activities help you learn what kinds of information the best, rather than putting yourself into one of the boxes listed above, never to be allowed out again!

What is your learning style?
We are going to try to identify your preferred learning styles so that you can use these to best effect in your revision. In order to do this, you will have to reflect on all of your learning to date and take a look through all your notes. Write down your answers to the questions in the table provided in the workbook. You can download the workbook from www.lifemoreextraordinary.com/workbook.

1. Look back at where you identified your strengths and weaknesses. Your first task is to identify how you were taught, or how you learned for each of these areas.
2. Now think about which lessons and learning experiences you have enjoyed most in the last year or so. Write down the top three to five.
3. Can you see any connections between how you were learning your strengths? Are there any connections between how you were learning your weaknesses? What are these connections?

I'll give you some examples.

If you are studying history, you may have had a role play discussion where different members of the class took on different characters from history and had to represent their point of view. Was this a successful learning experience for you? What was successful about it? What can you remember best about it? What were your dominant feelings and emotions during this experience?

If you are studying biology, you may have performed a dissection. Was this a successful learning experience for you? What was successful about it? What can you remember best about it? What were your dominant feelings and emotions during this experience?

If you are studying art, you may have visited an art gallery. Was this a successful learning experience for you? What was successful about it? What can you remember best about it? What were your dominant feelings and emotions during this experience?

Some things you might like to think about when you're identifying how you successfully learn are:

- Were you working alone or with one or more other people? What was it about this situation that helped you to learn? Were the actual people you were learning with important, or was it just about having other people to share the learning experience with?
- Were you actively involved in the learning experience? Were you doing the dissection, playing a part, engaging your mind to ask questions or analyse information?
- Were pictures, diagrams or images a big part of the learning experience. For example, if a scientific phenomenon is being explained to you, do you understand it better by reading a written description or looking at a diagram?
- Does having sound, music or the spoken word help you to remember things?
- Is it all about reading and talking with you? Is there nothing better than a book full of written information as far as you're concerned?
- Were you using logic, reasoning and systems to understand something e.g. a leads to b, which leads to c.
- Where were you when you were learning? Were you at home, in school, outside, inside, on the sofa, in bed, at a desk?

Fill in the table – how do you learn best?

You can get a printable copy of this table at www.lifemoreextraordinary.com/workbook.

Top 5 Most Successful Learning Experiences	5 Least Successful Learning Experiences
1.	1.
2.	2.
3.	3.
4.	4.
5.	5.

Once you have a strong idea of how you most successfully learn, you can apply this to the revision techniques that you use. I hope it's obvious that you should scrap the ways of learning that didn't work for you.

It is important to remember that some subjects lend themselves better to certain learning styles. So, for English and History visual and social learning are much easier to use whereas in the sciences using images for diagrams and logic are much more prevalent.

Your challenge is how to incorporate your favourite learning styles into the subjects that you need to revise, and particularly how to use them to improve your weaknesses, and even possibly make them your strengths. For example, if you had a role play about global warming where each person in the class presented a different country's point of view and you remember all those views particularly well, how could you replicate this learning experience in your revision? Maybe, if you're studying a period of history where the views of different people are important for you to remember, you could write a cheat sheet summarising the argument of each person. You could then act it out to yourself, or get friends or family members involved.

You need to be creative in how you transfer the success of one learning experience to another area.

I'll give you a hint though, the more actively you engage with the information the better you will remember it (and you'll have more fun, who said revision wasn't fun?). So, read it out loud, write it out over and over again, act it out, write a summary or cheat-sheet, teach someone else. All of these are active ways to engage with what you're learning, but the more active, the better! And, bear in mind, you don't have to make revision notes to be good at revising. One of my clients achieved 10 A*s and 2 As in her GCSEs without making any revision notes at all! She had identified her most successful ways of learning and used those, extremely effectively, to get outstanding results.

'You don't learn to walk by following rules.
You learn by doing, and by falling over.'
Richard Branson

How to create a revision timetable

'Spectacular achievement is always preceded
by unspectacular preparation.'
Robert H. Schuller

Anyone with a large piece of work to do needs a plan for how they're going to complete it. Whether they're a writer wanting to write a 50,000-word novel or a civil engineer wanting to build a new road, a plan is essential.

Your revision plan should take into account two key things:

1. What you need to know for your exam (basically, everything you need to revise)
2. How much time you have to do it in

You then allocate each topic that you need to revise to a time slot. Start with your weaknesses first. Before we dive into the details about how to create a revision plan, we should think first about when you should start your revision.

When to start your revision

In step 6, we talked about creating a daily habit of doing five minutes of revision, right from the beginning of the school year. If you start doing this right away the benefits will quickly build up. If you're having tests or mock exams throughout the school year then you should be revising for these as you go along.

However, the main body of your revision should start somewhere between Christmas and February half-term. I always feel that those who really knuckle down to their revision during February half-term are the ones who are ahead of the game and don't suffer from exam stress in the way that people who start their revision later sometimes do.

You should carry on devoting a portion of every day to revision from February half-term onwards. You will find that as you get to the end of the course content that is being taught in class you'll have less and less homework so that you can focus more of your attention on your revision. This means that by Easter, the vast majority of your study time is spent on revision.

During the Easter holiday you should, again, like in February, really focus on your revision and independent study. These days, when you don't have exam leave leading up to your exams, these three weeks of school holiday (half-term and Easter) are the only times when you have the time and freedom to get stuck into your own independent revision. You need to make the most of these opportunities.

Of course, during the school holidays you should also be taking time to rest, relax and build up your strength for the coming term. However, you must always keep in mind your vision and your goals so that you get the work done to achieve them.

Step-by-step instructions on how to make a revision plan:

1. Know what you need to know

Earlier in this chapter, I told you to find the syllabus or specification for every subject that you're studying. These are the documents on which you're going to base your revision plan.

2. Know the dates of your exams

In the UK, exams are usually in May and June, unless you're taking retakes. The closer you get to the time of the exams the more likely a final date and time for each subject and syllabus will be published. Again, ask your teacher for this information or the exams office at your school.

3. Identify your strengths and weaknesses

Ensure that you've identified your strengths and weaknesses, as I advised you to do earlier in the chapter.

4. Make a revision plan outline

Make a really simple weekly outline on a piece of paper, with the days of the week along the long side and the times of the day (or just morning, afternoon and evening) along the short side. Make enough copies of this to last you up until your exams are finished. It might be easiest to do this on the computer and print it out. Or, you can use the revision plan outline in the workbook (www.lifemoreextraordinary.com/workbook). However, you must not be afraid to make your own, adapted to your own particular needs.

5. Mark your exams onto your revision plan

You know the dates and times of your exams because you asked your teacher. This is the first information you need to add to your revision timetable.

6. Add on your subject areas

Now you can add in the subject areas you need to study. I would recommend putting the subject areas you're least confident with first (the weaknesses you identified with red, amber and green before). I would also recommend colour-coding your timetable. So, for example, if you're studying biology and you're not at all confident in your understanding of meiosis and mitosis, put them early on the revision timetable and colour them in with your colour for biology, let's say green. You need to add in all the different things you highlighted when you looked through the syllabus.

Once you've added all the things you're not confident about you can put in things you're much more comfortable with. It is very important to prioritise your weaknesses on your revision timetable - you stand to gain the most marks by focusing on your weaknesses rather than your strengths.

7. Build in breaks and real-life

You have to schedule regular breaks into your revision. This is important so that your brain gets a rest, you don't get bored and you stay happy and healthy. However, you need to be purposeful with your breaks. In shorter breaks, maybe plan to have a cup of tea and a snack. In longer breaks, plan to get some exercise or catch up with your friends. Don't just switch over to *Facebook*, forget you're supposed to be revising and waste away hours. We'll talk more about revision breaks in the next chapter.

8. Use a timer to keep you on track

Schedule your revision in blocks that make sense to you. Never sit for more than an hour without a short break. You may also want to switch topic areas quite frequently to make sure you get through everything and you keep your mind fresh. Use a timer to keep you on track with this. So, set a timer for an hour. When it goes off set it for five minutes, or ten minutes, however long this break is scheduled to be so that you're reminded to come back to your task. If you don't want to use the timer on your phone because of the potential for distractions, use a kitchen timer or the timer on a digital clock or watch.

9. Get someone to hold you accountable

Ask someone you trust, a parent, friend, brother, sister or mentor, to hold you accountable for sticking to your timetable. At the beginning of each day tell them, show them or email them exactly what you're planning to do. At the end of the day, report back to them to say how you did. You can also talk to them about how it went, what went well and what was difficult; this might help you trouble-shoot for the next day.

10. Tick things off as you go

Ticking things off a list can give you a wonderful sense of achievement. As you go along, tick each topic area off the revision plan or off your syllabus. Doing this will help your confidence grow as you approach the exam, so you can walk into the exam hall knowing you're fully prepared and ready for whatever is in that exam paper.

If you'd like to be guided through the process of making a revision timetable in a more step-by-step, day-by-day way then you can join my free 5-day email course called the Revision Planning Kickstarter. Sign up for it here: http://www.lifemoreextraordinary.com/revision-planning-kickstarter/.

Revision Plan Outline

	Monday	Tuesday	Wednesday	Thursday	Friday	Saturday	Sunday
Morning							
Afternoon							
Evening							

Subject key

Subject	Colour	Subject	Colour	Subject	Colour

Now that you know what it takes to pass this exam, how to identify which skills and areas of knowledge you need to focus on, how to decide which revision techniques you should be using and how to create a revision timetable it's time to get on with your revision! In the next chapter, I'll give you some more practical hints and tips about how to revise, how to stay motivated and focused and how to spend your revision breaks so that they actually help you to learn.

Chapter Summary

- The first step towards doing really well in an exam is to know what knowledge and skills you will be examined on. Find out by getting a copy of the syllabus or specification or asking your teacher for a complete checklist of what you need to know.
- Once you know the complete range of knowledge and skills you'll need to know for the exam you need to decide which ones to focus on in your revision. Go through the list and identify your strengths and weaknesses. You should start your revision with your weaknesses as these are the areas from which, by investing time and effort, you will gain the most improvement.
- Reflect on your past learning experiences to find out how you learn best and how you enjoy learning. Be creative about adapting these learning techniques to your revision. You'll be surprised to find out that you don't actually have to make a forest of revision notes to do very successful revision.
- Create a revision timetable that prioritises your weaknesses. Planning out your revision helps you to keep on track so that you make the most of the time leading up to your exam. It's much easier to get going if you know what you need to do when you sit down at your desk to revise.

Step 9

Revision: getting it done

'If you are not willing to learn, no one can help you. If you are determined to learn, no one can stop you.'
Unknown.

This chapter includes:

- How to revise like a movie director
- The single best way to revise
- 40 other ways to revise
- How to create an environment for successful revision
- How to get through the revision and not procrastinate or get stuck on one thing

Once you've planned your revision you're ready to get started. This step is all about getting your revision done, and just keeping on going until you get to the end of exam season.

Revise like a movie director

Movie directors, so I'm led to believe, rarely get the best footage in the first take. Students revising for exams rarely achieve the best understanding or the greatest recall of a subject after only one viewing. This means that you've got to put the time in, and aim to go over every piece of knowledge on the syllabus at least three times in the revision process. Typically this might look like:

- Take 1 – make revision notes summarising your class notes
- Take 2 – read over revision notes out loud a week later
- Take 3 – summarise your revision notes still further onto index cards, flash cards or posters

The point is, every time you return to this information your mind will become more and more familiar with it. In many ways, you should be aiming to do even more takes than this. For example:

- Take 1 – make revision notes summarising your class notes and read them through out loud before you stop work for that day
- Take 2 – flick through the notes you made yesterday before starting a new set of revision notes, just to spark your memory
- Take 3 – when you've finished a module of notes get someone to test you on them. Identify which areas you are still finding it difficult to explain or remember
- Take 4 – summarise the areas you were finding difficult onto index cards, flash cards or posters
- Take 5 – read through the index cards, flash cards or posters again and test yourself
- Take 6 – get someone to test you again. Identify the areas of weakness that remain and work on them some more
- And so on....

Remember, you don't necessarily have to be using revision notes, flash cards, index cards etc. Always use the methods that best serve your learning styles, as explained in step 8. I've just used these things to illustrate the point that you need to repeat yourself over and over again, that's the 're' part of 'revision'.

The Power Hour

I was using this revision technique years ago when I was at university to great effect but I hadn't given it a name. However, I first heard the term 'Power Hour' from Martin Griffin, co-author of *The A Level Mindset*. When I was at university I would choose a topic to revise that day and choose a past-paper question on that topic. I'd then revise the content I would need to answer that question. Finally, I would do the past-paper under timed conditions then hand it in to my supervisor who would mark it and give me feedback. It was an incredibly effective way to revise and I wish that I'd discovered it years before.

How to revise effectively for GCSE and A Levels

Before we dive into this technique in detail let's think about where people go wrong with their revision. Are you ready?

- They spend far too much time revising content and not enough time practicing their exam technique
- They use revision techniques that don't work very well for them
- They try to revise for too long in one sitting and lose focus
- They use passive revision techniques (like reading their text book) rather than active revision techniques

The beautiful thing about the revision Power Hour is that it addresses all of these problems head-on.

This is what the revision Power Hour does for you:

- Forces you to balance the time between learning the content and practicing your exam technique
- Stops you from spending too long in one sitting on revision techniques that don't work. You mix up your activities to make it more likely you'll remember stuff when you've finished your revision session.
- You don't have to revise for too long. It's a maximum of one hour, but you can break it down into 20-minute chunks with

five-minute breaks between each session. (Although you can extend it for essay-based subjects like English literature).

- You're forced to use an active revision technique; writing down what you know and analysing your work to see how many marks you've earned.

In addition to these benefits, the revision Power Hour works by:

- Encouraging you to get feedback from your teacher about the things you're struggling with
- Helping you to think about how you can continually improve to raise your grade
- Making you repeat the things you're learning in different ways so you're more likely to remember them.

How do you do a Power Hour?

Have a good look at the infographic before reading on. You can get a downloadable, poster-size version of this infographic in the workbook. Stick this on the inside of your folder to carry around with you, or pin it on your bedroom wall. Remember, you can download the workbook from www.lifemoreextraordinary.com/workbook.

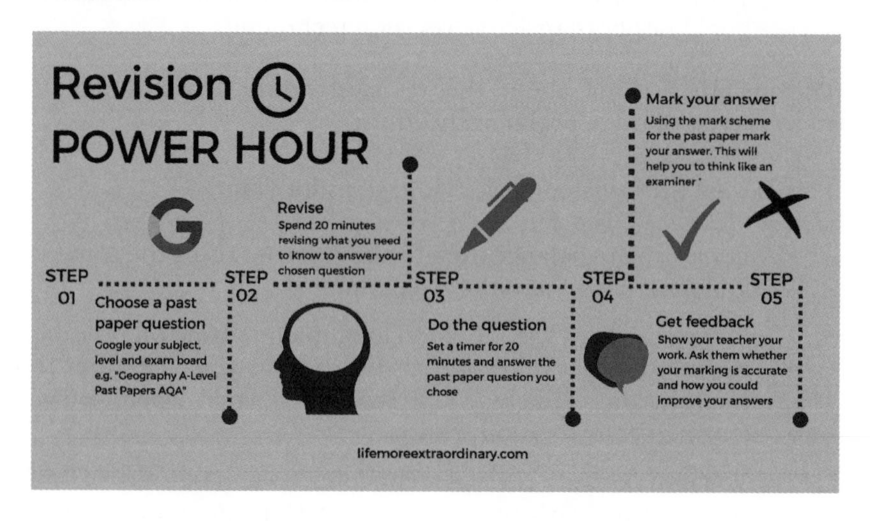

Step-by-step intructions for a Power Hour

1. Choose a past paper question

First, you need to find a past paper question to answer (and the mark scheme). You'll use Google to do this. You can find a link to a video I made about how to find past paper questions and mark schemes in the workbook.

Pro tip: spend some time printing off all the past paper questions for each subject and filing them neatly so you've got them to hand.

2. Revise

Set a timer and spend 20 minutes revising what you need to know to answer the question you've chosen. This might be anything from quotes for your closed book English exam to facts for science or geography.

Use the revision techniques you've identified as being most successful for you, or pick one of the forty techniques I've listed later in this step.

3. Do the question

Set the timer again for 20 minutes and answer the past paper question you chose. You might find that you need different lengths of time according to the subject you're revising and the length of the question. For example, for English Literature you might need a whole hour to do an essay-style question. For other subjects you might only need ten minutes. Adjust the length of time to the amount of time you'd spend in an actual exam answering questions worth that number of marks.

4. Mark your answer

Use the mark scheme you found in step 1 to mark your work.

This step is crucial and I can't emphasise it enough. I can't tell you the number of students who come to me saying that they are doing hundreds of past-paper questions but their marks never improve. You will only improve your marks if you learn to think like an examiner. Marking your own work is how you learn to think like an examiner.

What you gain from marking your work is the ability to read and analyse your work the way an examiner does. You have to be able to see your work the way your examiner sees it in order to see where improvements can be made.

It is difficult and puts you way outside your comfort zone looking at your own work in this critical and different way. However, there is nothing that you can do in your revision that will be more important in terms of increasing your marks. Don't skip this step!

5. Get feedback

If you're unsure of how accurate your marking is or you want to know how you can improve show your work to your teacher. Ask them for feedback on how to improve.

Again, this step is really important if you want to make continuous improvements to your exam technique, and therefore your marks, during the revision period. It is also really helpful in building your confidence in your own ability to analyse your work, think like an examiner and mark accurately.

What if I run out of past papers?

This can happen if you do a lot of power hours, or if your exam specification is very new and there aren't many past papers yet.

However, when you've done that many past papers you're in a great position. By now, you should be able to think like an examiner and it will be easy to invent your own questions.

Learn to think like the chief examiner

It is possible to go beyond thinking like an examiner, and learn to think like a chief examiner. There are two reasons you will want to do this:

1. So that you have an even deeper insight into the way an examiner's mind works
2. You are able to predict the kind of questions that might come up in your exam

3. If you run out of past paper questions you can invent your own to carry on practicing your exam technique.

Let me show you how to start thinking like a chief examiner and start writing your own practice questions. Use the worked examples and the worksheet in the workbook to help you go through this process for the first time.

1. Choose a type of exam question that you're going to focus on. You could choose a short answer question or an essay.
2. Find as many examples of this type of question as possible and write them down.
3. Highlight, circle or underline the command words in each question. Look carefully at how each question is structured. (See below for an explanation of command words and to see 28 of the most common ones used in exams).
4. Now, create some questions of your own, based on your knowledge of the specification or syllabus. Try to phrase them in the same way as the questions you wrote down above but use different subject areas.
5. Now answer your questions, then use your knowledge of the mark scheme to answer them. You will find in most mark schemes that there is a generic section as well as answers to specific questions set. Use the generic section as your guide to marking your own questions.

When you do revision power hours consistently you will soon see your marks and your confidence increase. You'll be walking into all your exams with your head held high, impatient to show off what you can do!

Command words

A command is an instruction, it tells you what to do. If you've got a dog and you say 'Sit!' that is a command. Every exam question contains a command word, or a short string of words, that tell you how the examiner wants you to answer the question.

Short answer question command words

Many exams start with short-answer questions that are worth between one and four marks. These are some typical command words that are used in these short-answer questions.

- **Mark with an arrow** – usually there will be a picture, diagram, photograph or graph. You need to draw an arrow to point to the thing you're being asked for, and possibly label it. You will usually be asked for the same number of arrows as the number of marks available.
- **Label** – once again, there will often be a picture, diagram, photograph or graph. Use a line or an arrow, if appropriate, to show a place in the graphic and use the correct word to describe it. You may also see empty boxes where you need to put the labels. You will usually be asked for the same number of labels as the number of marks available.
- **Draw** – use a pencil to draw whatever you're being asked for. This might be a graph, a diagram, a table, a sketch. If appropriate use labels as well to prove your knowledge to the examiner.
- **Complete** – there will be an incomplete sentence, table, graph, diagram or something else. Add in the numbers or words, or finish off drawing, whatever it is.
- **Measure** – most usually a science, maths or geography question. You need to measure something. If a scale is given e.g. on a map, pay special attention to it and the units when giving your answer.
- **Calculate** – use a formula in maths or science, or simple maths in other subjects, to work out a sum.
- **Predict** – in short answer form, this will often require you to look at some numbers, or a graph, and say what the next number or data point will be.
- **Show** – work out an answer but show how you got to the answer, often used in maths.
- **Work out** – pretty much the same as calculating the answer.
- **Estimate** – you don't need to give an exact answer here but it's a good idea to show how you arrived at your answer.

Longer answer questions: simple command words

When questions are worth more than three marks, what is asked of you becomes a bit more complicated. These command words will typically be used for questions worth between three and eight marks.

- **Describe** – you are being asked to write down in words any of these things: what something looks like, how something works or how a character feels. You are not being asked to explain, that's something different.
- **Give X examples/reasons** – this question is really helping you if it gives a number. If you're being asked for three reasons or examples and there are six marks available, each reason is worth two marks. This tells you that you need to give your reason and then go into a little more detail.
- **What evidence is there to support** – from your knowledge, or from the materials (such as sources, a text, map or graph) that you're given in the exam find some information that supports the idea in the question.
- **Which is the correct** – you're given options and you must choose the right one.

Longer answer questions: more complex command words

Longer answer questions are worth from about six marks upwards. These questions are typically marked in a different way to short answer questions. Instead of being given a mark for every correct point you make, you are level-marked. This means the examiner is looking for certain qualities in your work, alongside your knowledge. This might be how well you structure your answer into paragraphs, how often you give examples to back up your points, or any number of factors.

To achieve real success in this kind of question you need to practice over and over again, and get inside the head of the examiner (we've talked about how to do this already). To do this, get copies of the mark scheme and learn how to mark your own work.

- **Explain** – the most popular command in this category. This is going a step beyond describing, so instead of just saying what something looks like or how something happens, you're saying why it looks like that, or why it happens like that. Use phrases like 'this is because' to make it clear to the examiner that you're explaining.

- **Outline** - this could be as simple as describing something but is also used as a way to ask you to give a shortened explanation of something. E.g. 'Outline the reasons for the start of World War I' – you can't really do this in an exam length essay. You can hardly do it in a book, so the question is acknowledging that all they can reasonably ask for is an over-view.
- **Why** - this is pretty similar to explain.
- **What is meant by** – this could be as simple as giving a definition, or it could be as complex as being given a quote and discussing it in detail. It depends on the number of marks available for the question.
- **Suggest** – this is explaining or giving reasons why.
- **Suggest one advantage of X over Y** - this is quite a helpful question as it's asking you to specifically compare two things. It shouldn't be hard to answer this question very directly.
- **Would you recommend** – this is looking for you to give your opinion, and explain your opinion, with sufficient knowledge or evidence.
- **Analyse** – this question could just as easily say compare, contrast or explain. It literally means 'examine in detail'.
- **How far was X due to Y** – once again, this is quite a helpful one. It's giving you two things to consider, but you need to analyse what you know about how they're connected and give your answer.
- **How successful was** – another analysis type of question.
- **Evaluate** - another analysis type of question.
- **Contrast / Compare** – look at one thing and say how it's similar and different to another thing.

- **Discuss** – either put forward two points of view, compare them and say which one you think is correct, or put forward the point of view you agree with, explain why and why you don't agree with alternative points of view.
- **Provide evidence** - from what you know, or from the information you've been provided in the exam, give examples of something.

Practice makes perfect

In order to really understand what these command words mean, and how you should interpret them in your exam, you need to do lots and lots of past papers and power hours are the perfect way to do this. Once you know what the examiner is looking for in every type of question, you will be in the best position ever to ace your exams!

40 ways to revise

In step 8, you identified how you learn most successfully. However, sometimes you need a change to keep your revision fresh and interesting or you find that a technique is no longer working for you or you can't make it work for one of your subjects. To help you with this, I've listed forty different methods you can use to revise. Look through them, find the ones that have worked best for you up until now and decide which others you're going to try to see if they work, based on your most successful learning styles.

1. Mind maps or spider diagrams
2. Use index cards to write the topic on one side and summarise it in bullet points on the other
3. Use post-it notes
4. Use posters to make a diagram or summary of a module and stick it above your desk, or on the back of the toilet door, or somewhere else where you'll see it often
5. Complete online quizzes - there are lots of apps and websites for this
6. Quizzes that you design yourself or with a friend
7. Get someone to test you such as a classmate, sibling or parent

8. Test yourself
9. Revision notes – a summary version of your original notes
10. Draw a diagram
11. Flash cards are great for learning vocabulary words in a foreign language, or key technical terms in science or the social sciences. Write the English word / keyword or draw a picture on one side, and the definition / foreign language word on the other. You can also use apps to make flash cards
12. Make an audio recording and listen back to it on a walk or run or on the bus
13. Make a video
14. Make a game
15. Play the game 'Just a Minute' – inspired by the Radio 4 panel show, try to talk on the subject for one minute without hesitation, deviation or repetition
16. Listen to a podcast about the subject
17. Watch a TV programme about the subject
18. Watch a YouTube video or DVD about the subject
19. Watch an animation of the idea
20. Draw a diagram
21. Create a mnemonic, e.g. 'Richard of York Gave Battle in Vain' for the colours of the rainbow: red, orange, yellow, green, blue, indigo and violet. This is best for lists of information, particularly information that needs to be memorised in a particular order. It's not good for complicated subjects or arguments
22. Highlight your notes
23. Watch a film or TV drama on the subject – this is particularly good for subjects like English and history
24. Find a different text book on the subject to see if their explanation means more to you than the textbook you've already got
25. Look it up on the internet

26. Read it out loud to yourself over and over again
27. Write out the information over and over again
28. Discuss the work with a friend or classmate – this is great for complex concepts. Each take one side of the argument and try to argue each other down. You have to have a strong grasp of both sides of the argument to be successful
29. Write a condensed argument both for and against an idea or concept
30. Invent essay titles based on the content of your syllabus and the structure of past essay titles
31. Write an essay plan
32. Do examples, e.g. using formulae for maths, chemistry or physics.
33. Compose a song, this can help with foreign languages, or help to get a series of events to stick in your mind
34. Write a poem or limerick – this can help with difficult vocabulary, helping you remember definitions, or to remember a series of events.
35. When you can't sit at your desk a moment longer – go on a visit to a place connected with what you're studying e.g. if you're studying Tudor history visit Hampton Court Palace, if you're studying astrophysics go to the National Space Centre, if you're studying politics go on a guided tour of the House of Commons
36. Act it out – you could use this for anything from a five minute version of Hamlet where you play all the characters, to how sub-atomic particles change position in the atomic structure
37. Model using play-dough or modelling clay to show the different stages in a process. For example, in geography you could show the different stages in the formation of a stack in models
38. Teach someone else – the ultimate proof of whether you understand something is whether you can successfully make someone else understand it. So, find someone who

doesn't know what you're learning and teach them. A parent, younger sibling, grandparent or friend doing a different subject – anyone who's game to learn something new

39. Understand what different command words in exam questions mean e.g. describe, explain, discuss and calculate
40. Do Power Hours - I know I've said this already, but everyone should be doing Power Hours

An environment for successful revision

Acing your exams isn't just about how you revise, but where you revise. It's really important to create an environment that will help rather than hinder your learning - this comes back to some of the things we talked about in step 6 about good habit formation. If your environment makes it easy for you to stick to your good revision habits and hard for you to break them then you are far more likely to keep on track with your revision.

Where you sit

Start with where you sit. I'd thoroughly recommend sitting at a desk, it's the most ergonomic thing to do when you're working with pen and paper most of the time (ergonomic means the most comfortable and appropriate thing for your whole body). Make sure your chair is comfortable and it's at the right height for the desk; you don't want to get crippling aches from being in an unnatural position for too long. To avoid strain on your back, always sit up straight with your heels directly under your knees. Never sit with one knee crossed over the other. If you're sitting in an easy chair, it's OK to slouch so long as your whole back is supported.

If sitting at a desk doesn't work for you, be honest about what does. If you sit on the bed, do you get drowsy, or do your dreams become too full of your revision and prevent you from getting a proper night's rest? I'm not going to judge you for where you decide to revise, your exam results will do that for you, you just need to be really honest about what suits you best.

You might find that if you always revise in the same place you begin to feel trapped. Try moving around the house if you begin to feel like this or if you feel too confined in your house, try revising in a library or even at a friend's or relative's house. It can really help to get out of your own home as there are many fewer distractions when you don't have all your own things around you.

Background noise

Does it help you to have the radio on in the background so you don't feel alone? Do you like to sit at the kitchen table with the family buzzing around you so you don't feel cut off from the world by revision? Or, does your mind need complete silence in order to be able to process all the information that you're feeding it. I know my requirements have changed over the years in this respect. When I was 16, I listened to music on the radio while I revised. By the time I was 18 I needed silence most of the time, but sometimes I liked to go in the garden with the family. At university, my friends and I would make use of the glorious summer weather that students invariably miss in exam season and lie on blankets in the gardens while we all revised.

Your needs in this area can change hour by hour, day by day and year by year. Just be in tune with yourself and assess whether the environment you're in is working for you.

I would never recommend anyone to watch TV while revising, unless you're purposefully watching a programme connected with your subject, you're taking notes and paying proper attention. The combination of noise and pictures is just too distracting for your poor brain trying to take in all that information.

Blocking out other distractions

There are countless other distractions; social media is a terrible one for interrupting you, as are phone calls and text messages. You could turn off notifications on your phone, leave your phone on the other side of the room or even just outside the door. You can check your phone during your breaks, if that's what you prefer to do.

What other distractions stop you from focusing on revision? Be honest with yourself, write them down and then try to come up with a solution to prevent those distractions from getting in the way of your revision. This revision time is extremely precious, it is make or break time for your grades, and therefore your big dream.

Use the table in the workbook (www.lifemoreextraordinary.com/workbook) to help you to identify your distractions and come up with solutions to them.

Are you a lark or an owl?

Some folks are morning people and others are evening types. I have always found that I am a morning person, the earlier in the day I start, the more I get done. Find out what suits you best and try to work with it, rather than against it. Also, try to establish revision hours that fit with normal school hours at the weekend and in the holidays so that you don't disrupt your sleep patterns.

What are you drinking?

Keep yourself hydrated while you revise with a glass of water, try not to consume too many sugary or caffeinated drinks. They may give you a boost in the short term, but after every sugar high comes a low and that will detract from your revision. Stop every once in a while for a proper break, maybe a cup of tea with a friend or member of your family, but go back to work with your glass of water.

How to stay motivated and focused

One of the hardest things about revision is staying motivated and focused and just keeping on going. It is tiring, it is draining and it does take you away from some of the things you enjoy in life. However, it's important. I'm going to give you some helpful strategies to keep you motivated so that you can keep revising even when you're bored, fed-up and can't be bothered.

Keep your eye on the prize

Think back to step 1 where you identified your dream, or great big 'why'. When you get up feeling all dopey, lacking energy and you just can't be bothered, think about that dream. Look at your vision board, or read your journal. Think about how wonderful life is going to be when you achieve your great big 'why'. Close your eyes and take a minute to visualise the life you dream of. Are you really willing to sacrifice your dream because you're feeling a little bit lazy today?

Break your revision down into bite-sized chunks

One of the biggest mistakes I see people making with revision is trying to concentrate for far too long. You should never try to sit at your desk concentrating for more than an hour at a time. However, you might find your optimum length of time for concentration is much shorter than this. The minimum time you should try to concentrate for is 20 minutes. The thing is, you need to decide how long you're going to revise for and focus on it completely for that length of time. Shut out distractions and be strong to stay focused. Once that time has elapsed you can stand-up and have a break.

The best way to manage this is to use a timer. One of the things I recommend to my clients is to use the timer on their phone. Set the amount of time you want to focus for then leave the phone on the other side of the room, or even just outside the door, so that you can hear it when it goes off but you can't see it. It's also a good idea to set it to silent so you don't hear or notice when you get messages or alerts. Leaving it on the other side of the room also forces you to get up at the end of the revision session to turn off the alarm - this enforced movement is good for your brain and your learning!

Identify your mini-motivations

Many people find it hard to sit down and get started with their revision because there are other more fun things to do, like scrolling through *Facebook*, watching their favourite TV programme, playing a computer game or phoning a friend. What I suggest you do is reverse your psychology; instead of letting these prevent you from doing your work turn them into incentives. So, for example, you could say to yourself that if you do 45 minutes of revision you're allowed ten minutes on *Facebook*. Or, if you do three hours revision in total this evening, with smaller breaks interspersed, you can watch your favourite TV programme when you've finished, which you might have recorded so that you don't have to disrupt your work flow to watch it.

You need to identify a range of mini-motivations that take different lengths of time. Try to identify five five-minute mini-motivations, five ten-minute mini-motivations and five 30-60 minute mini-motivations. Use the dedicated page in the workbook (www.lifemoreextraordinary.com/workbook) to write these down.

Here are some ideas for mini-motivations:

- Five minutes - make a cup of tea, do sit-ups, walk round the garden, play with your dog
- Ten minutes - a brisk walk around the block, check social media, watch a YouTube video
- 30-60 minutes - do a workout, go for a run, watch TV, phone a friend

Every time you sit down for a revision session decide how long you're going to focus for and what you're going to reward yourself with at the end. Then, set your timer and get to work!

Find an accountability partner

Social accountability really helps. Do you remember in step 6 where I talked about the different habits personalities? If you're the kind of person who needs to be accountable to someone this will really help you to stay on track. It's something that I offer to my private clients and it really helps to keep them focused to have someone to report into every day, or even every hour. You need to share your revision timetable with your accountability partner. Your partner could be a parent, your best friend, your aunty, a sibling, or even me! It's probably best not to use your dog.

At the beginning of each day or study session, let them know what you're aiming to achieve. You can tell them if you live in the same house as them, email them or text them, whatever works for you. Then, you just need to work your way through your plan. You can keep them updated as you go e.g. sending them a message after every 20-60 minute study session, or you can just report to them at the very end to tell them how it's gone. If it's gone well then let them praise you. If you've had problems concentrating or understanding talk through what went wrong with them so that you can do better next time.

If you have an accountability partner your own age you might like to study together. Sometimes it's easier to stay focused when you're not suffering from the fear of missing out. If you can see them studying hard beside you you'll know that they're not out having fun so you can stay focused too.

Flex your will power muscle

At the end of the day, studying hard for exams over a period of weeks and months isn't always a bundle of laughs. You're not always going to feel motivated, no matter how hard you try to remember your great big 'why', come up with mini-motivations or use a partner to keep you accountable. Sometimes you just need to summon up the will power, grit your teeth and get on with what needs to be done.

This is where it's so important to look after yourself properly, like we talked about in step 3. If you haven't had enough sleep, you're hungry or your muscles are twitching because you haven't had enough exercise this week you'll find it much harder to flex your will power muscle. So, for the sake of making all this easier for yourself, make sure you're getting a good night's sleep every night, you're eating well and you take regular exercise.

> *'Willpower is the key to success. Successful people strive no matter what they feel by applying their will to overcome apathy, doubt or fear.'*
> Dan Millman

Revision breaks

We've already talked about mini-motivations and breaking your revision up into bite sized chunks. I just wanted to emphasise the importance of taking well planned revision breaks. There are many, many advantages to taking revision breaks, so long as you're earning them by doing a decent amount of revision in the first place.

The advantages of revision breaks

- Revision breaks give your brain a rest. When you're revising for a longer period of time (45 to 60 minutes) you'll find your brain getting tired and that you're having to work extra hard to concentrate and take information in. This is a sure sign that you need a revision break. If you take five to ten minutes away from your learning you'll come back refreshed and ready to learn more.

- You won't get bored with your revision as easily as you're breaking it up by moving around and doing different activities.
- You can carry on with some of your hobbies and interests e.g. playing the piano or sports so you don't feel like you're having to give up everything for your exams
- They're good for your mind and body as they encourage you to move and think about something else.

Why you need to move during your revision breaks
When you take a break from your revision you should be aiming to do something as different as possible from studying. Get out of your chair (or off your bed), away from your desk and preferably out of the room where you've been studying. For best results, get active in your revision break.

By getting your heart rate going and giving your brain something completely different to think about you will be giving yourself a proper break. You'll return to your books with endorphins flowing through your veins, feeling energised and ready to revise again.

Contrast this with staying at your desk scrolling on your phone and you should be able to see how much more effective an active revision break is for helping with your learning. If you don't believe me - try it and see how much better you feel and how much more effectively you revise afterwards!

25+ active revision break ideas

Go cardio!

- Go for a run
- Go for a walk
- Go for a cycle
- Get on a cross-trainer
- Go for a swim

Exercises – free standing

- Press-ups
- Squats
- Plank
- Jumping jacks
- Jumping lunges

Garden games

- Skip with a rope
- Catch
- Football
- Scatch
- Hopscotch

Household chores

- Mow the lawn
- Hoover
- Hang the washing on the line (outside)
- Clean the windows
- Sweep the patio

Exercises using household equipment

- Run up and down the stairs
- Tricep dips (on the edge of the bath, coffee table or chair)
- Chair step-ups
- Cans of food to do weights
- Sumo squats with a large bag of pasta, flour (or your biggest text book!)

Yoga routines

Search for yoga routines on YouTube, such as sun salutations, for a gentle way to stretch and raise your heart rate in your revision break. You'll be able to find yoga routines ranging from ten minutes to over an hour, pick one that's the length of the break you're planning to take.

I'm sure you can think of your own ideas for active revision breaks too. Just make sure you move your body in some way, whether it's just walking around the room or a full-on workout, during every revision break that you take.

Chapter Summary

- You need to revise like a movie director and plan to go over everything you need to know for your exams at least three times. Repetition will help to secure the knowledge in your mind.
- Make Power Hours the core of your revision. They are fantastic because they help you to remember content, practice exam technique and learn to think like an examiner. There is no better way to revise effectively for your exams.
- If you run out of past papers, make your own using the technique I have shown you. This will help you to think like the chief examiner!
- Know your command words so that you can directly answer every question you're asked in an exam.
- Experiment with different ways to revise so you don't get stale and you're always using methods that work for you.
- Make sure the place where you revise is comfortable and without distractions so that you can fully focus on your revision.
- Motivate yourself by keeping your great big why in mind at all times and by using mini-motivations.
- Take regular, active revision breaks to keep your brain fresh and your body moving.

Step 10

Exam Time

'Your mind will answer most questions if you learn to relax and wait for the answer.'
William S. Burroughs

This chapter includes:

- How to make your final preparations in the week and day before your exams
- How to perform your very best once you step inside the exam room
- How to keep going throughout exam season

One week before the exam

If you've read the previous two steps, you should have been revising hard for several weeks now. By steadily working your way through a solid revision plan, focusing on improving your weaknesses and your exam technique by using Power Hours, you will have been feeling your confidence grow. But, what should you be focusing on in the last week before your exams? If you're well prepared already, the last week won't be that different to all the previous weeks. Here are the things you should be doing to prepare for your exams with one week to go.

1. Identify your strengths and weaknesses

If you've been following my revision planning advice you'll have identified your strengths and weaknesses ages ago. However, at this point it's worth going over that list again. You'll probably find that, if you've been busy bringing your weaknesses up to scratch, your strengths and weaknesses have changed in relation to each other.

At this stage, you should refocus your efforts on your remaining weaknesses.

2. Study in focused bursts and take breaks

By now you should know how long you can focus for before you take a break. This could be anything from 20 to 60 minutes. Keep using a timer to time your focused study sessions and time your breaks as well.

3. Choose a topic for each study session

Start each study session knowing what you're going to focus on in that time. Don't sit down aimlessly thinking 'I must get some revision done', but not actually knowing what you're going to study.

4. Finesse your exam technique

Hopefully, you've been doing lots of past papers for weeks but if you haven't, you can't leave it any longer. You now have to prioritise your exam technique.

Use Power Hours (see step 9 for all the details about how to do Power Hours) to help you learn content, do past papers and learn to think like an examiner in a focused way.

5. Get help with anything you still don't understand

Pester your teacher, find a different text book in the library or look it up online. It's your responsibility to make sure that you understand every aspect of the syllabus for every subject.

6. Get plenty of sleep

Traditionally people think that to prepare for exams you leave all your revision until the last couple of days, stay up all night and cram. This is the very worst way to prepare for your exams. If you've followed my advice in the previous nine steps you will have no need to do this.

The very last thing I want you to do in the week before your exams is to deprive yourself of sleep. Sleep is vital for making sure all that good learning you've been doing is fixed in your head. While you're asleep new connections are made in your brain, so if you skimp on sleep you're effectively cheating yourself out of the knowledge you've gained in your study sessions.

Having a good night's sleep is also vital if you want to stay alert and to be able to think quickly and creatively in the exam itself. Sometimes creatively thinking about how you can use what you know will earn you more marks than an extra hour of revision.

7. Eat well

Try to eat healthy meals and snacks. Feed your body with goodness the way you're feeding your mind with knowledge. You should have developed these healthy eating habits during the year, the key is not to let them drop just because your exams are next week. Now is the time when you need that healthy foundation the most.

8. Exercise

Scientists are always coming up with new proof that exercise helps your brain. It's indisputable that fresh air and exercise reduce stress and make you feel better. Even if you only go for a 20 minute walk every day make sure you keep your body moving and your blood flowing to help you to ease stress, absorb all the revision you're doing and look after your mental and physical health.

9. Know the logistics

You should already know, but if you don't, find out when and where all your exams are going to be. Also make a plan to get yourself there on time.

10. Relax!

I know that might sound ridiculous but you need to have some wind down time at the end of each day so that you sleep well. This will also stop you from feeling like a revision machine. Look back at step 3 and make sure you've planned in some relaxation and wind-down time at the end of every day, and during the day as well, so that you're relaxed and well rested for exam day.

The last 24 hours before your exam

The day before

During the daytime, the day before your exam, you should carry on with your revision plan or school timetable as already planned out. Try to emphasise revising for the exam the following day, but if you're in the middle of exam season with lots of exams still to take, it's probably not a good idea to exclusively focus on just the exam you've got tomorrow.

Just keep going at the revision, steadily and surely making progress.

The night before

The night before should be all about rest and relaxation. You might want to cast your eye gently over your revision notes or get someone to test you on something for one last time. However, hard-core brainwork should not be your emphasis. Here are some of the things that you should be doing:

- Double checking you have all your equipment for tomorrow's exam ready to go in the morning
- Having a nutritious and healthy meal
- Taking some exercise or getting some fresh air
- Relaxing in your favourite way, whether that's watching TV, having a bubble bath or hanging out with your friends
- Getting an early night and a fantastic night's sleep

Being relaxed and well rested is the healthiest way to prepare. It will mean that in the morning your mind is sharp, ready to dredge up everything you've revised, and nimble enough to make the most of what you know, even if you can't give the perfect answer to the question in front of you.

On the day of the exam

On the morning of the exam it's all about being organised and prepared. Follow some of these simple steps to make sure you arrive at your exam calm and confident.

- Set an alarm and have a back-up alarm (whether that's another alarm clock or a person willing to make sure you're up).
- Eat a filling and nutritious breakfast.
- Double-check you've got everything you need for the day.
- Have a back-up plan for how you're going to get to the exam, just in case your normal transport plan goes pear-shaped.
- Stay calm and focused. Use deep breathing and don't let other people's nervousness and insecurity get to you. Don't talk about the exam or how much revision you've done to your friends, it won't help your chances of success or your friendship.

In the exam hall

> *"An exam is not a test, it's the proof. If you've done the work you'll be okay."*
> Humphry Evatt

Make sure your desk doesn't wobble

This may sound like a ridiculous thing to put first, but just imagine how annoying it would be to spend three hours writing at a wobbly desk, both for you and all the other people around you. When you sit down give your desk a gentle shake to see if it wobbles. If it does, ask an invigilator to do something about it.

Read the instructions

By this point in time you should be very well aware of what is required of you in this exam. You should have done past papers with your teachers, mock exams and practice questions until you wish you'll never see another one. However familiar you think you are with what is required of you in this exam, read the instructions. Some small things may have changed since the last time this exam was set and you want to be on top of it. I have known students who thought they knew what to do in their exam, but achieved disappointing results simply because they didn't read the instructions beforehand.

Write your details on the paper

Whether they're asking for your name, candidate number, centre number or star sign (probably not that one!) make sure you give the exam board the information they need to identify you. If you forget to do this all your hard work will have been for nothing.

Allocate your time correctly

Make sure you allocate your time fairly across the number of marks available. In some exams you might have to do three essays in three hours. Assuming all the essays are worth the same number of marks, that's one essay per hour. But even when it's this easy you need to think about how much time you'll spend planning what you're going to say, how much time you'll spend writing and how much time you'll spend reading back and correcting what you've written.

In other exams where you have more short answer questions you need to calculate more carefully where and how you're going to spend your time. Count up the number of marks available and the number of minutes you have. Divide the number of minutes by the number of marks available. E.g. if 90 marks are available and you have an hour and a half for the exam that's 90 minutes divided by 90 marks – one mark per minute. You can keep track of how you're doing for time if you've planned this out.

Choose which questions you want to answer first

You don't have to do questions in the order they appear on the exam paper, the examiner will never know which order you did them in and wouldn't care if they did. You could choose to do a question that you feel really comfortable with first to build up your confidence. Or, you could do all the short-answer questions first to get those easy marks in the bank. However, you need to make sure you're still using your time allocation correctly.

Answer the question

As a teacher I can't tell you how many times I wrote 'ATQ' on a student's work. What does 'ATQ' stand for? 'Answer the question'.

This is of the utmost importance. If you don't directly answer the question you waste time and will lose marks.

How do you make sure you're answering the question? Read the question through and underline or circle command words. What are command words? They're the words telling you what to do. Refer back to step 9 for a thorough explanation of command words. Following this, you need to look at the more subject specific aspects of the question; there might be keywords, names of characters in a book, specific dates, a specific place, or you might be asked for a specific type of example. You need to make sure you're really well focused on what it is you're being asked for.

What if you think you can't give the information the question is asking for? Do your best. I can remember many a time where I didn't think I had a brilliant example or situation to write about, but I used what I knew and made it as applicable to the question as possible. I achieved straight A grades so it worked for me. You need to do the best you can with what you've got, and if you do it intelligently you'll be given credit for it. This is why you need to be as well rested and as alert as possible for you exam - so that you can think quickly and be creative with what you know.

Another thing you can do to make it clear to the examiner that you're answering the question is to sign-post your answer. For example, you might repeat the question back in your answer. If the question asks for three reasons you may split your answer up with sub-headings saying 'Reason 1', then giving your answer, before 'Reason 2' etc.

Don't panic

If you've done everything in the previous nine steps you should be brimming with confidence rather than panicking but there are some people who are prone to nervousness, however well prepared they are. If you do feel yourself start to panic try to do these things.

- Close your eyes and take three really deep breaths
- Push all negative thoughts away. You could come up with a mantra to repeat such as 'I can do this', or have a calming

image such as your favourite place or a family photo that you focus your mind on.

- Focus your mind on what you're doing in this moment rather than all the other things that might be crowding your mind. You'll have plenty of time for those thoughts once you leave the exam room.
- Get on with the task in hand!

Check your work

When you're planning out how to spend your time in the exam make sure you allow time to check your work. This is particularly important if there are marks available for spelling, punctuation and grammar. You also want to make sure that what you've written makes sense and is accurate. Checking your work and adding a few corrections could easily earn you another few marks, which is plenty to push you up a grade. Also, thoroughly check the exam paper to make sure you haven't missed a question: look on the back of the question booklet and check that you haven't turned over two pages at once. One of my clients had to re-take her maths GCSE simply because she forgot to turn the page over and do the last few questions on the back of the booklet. What a waste of time!

Don't be tempted to leave the exam early

Use all the time given to you. Sometimes this can mean you read through all your work five times. However, it can make you take the time to really think something through and thrash an idea out that you found difficult the first time you attempted a question. Try to spot the weaker areas of the exam paper and work on them if you have time leftover. In most exams you won't be penalised for writing down incorrect information so adding more and more to answers could well gain you extra marks.

If you really have nothing left to do, and you've checked your work so many times your eyes are crossed, count up the number of marks you think you've earned and have a go at predicting what grade you're going to get. If you've followed all my advice this little exercise should make you leave the exam hall with a smile on your face!

How to cope with two exams in one day

We can all remember that dreaded moment. The day you get your exam timetable and, there, right in the middle of all that stress and strain, you see **two exams in one day**.

How on earth are you going to cope with that?

I've had lots and lots of the readers of my blog contact me worrying about this exact problem. It isn't a nice problem to have, but I promise you that you'll get through it. I've been there and done that on several occasions.

Most memorably, I had three exams in two days for my finals at university. That was a grand total of nine hours of exams in two days. There were a total of four exams to examine me on my whole final year. The results I got from those four exams would be what my entire three years at university would be judged on for the rest of my life. I'm not going to lie to you; those two days were hell. After the last of the three exams my eyes were raw with tiredness, my brain felt like it had been rung out like a sponge and my arm was ready to drop off from all that writing.

Regardless, I got through it and, I've learned a thing or two about how to get through this kind of situation.

Here are my best tips on how to cope with two exams in one day.

1. **Be very well prepared.** As soon as you know that you'll be having two exams in one day you need to start planning for it. It's no use thinking that you'll cram on the evening before. It's also no use thinking you'll cram the evening following two exams in one day for an exam you might have the day after. You need to plan to make sure all that knowledge is firmly fixed in your head in advance so there is no last minute work to do.
2. **Be well organised.** You should aim to take as much stress and strain out of the day as possible by being well organised. Make sure you've got all the kit you need prepared well in

advance. Make sure you know where you've got to be and at what time. Make sure you've got a back-up plan for how to get to the exam if your transport goes wrong. Make sure you set an alarm and get someone to help you get out of bed in plenty of time so you're not rushing.

3. **Eat healthily and heartily,** both the night before and at breakfast, and make sure you get yourself a filling lunch in between the exams. You need food that's going to keep you full, and prevent your blood sugar from dipping part way through. It's hard to do your best when your body is struggling physically.
4. **Get a good night's sleep.** Make sure you stop revising early enough the night before so that your brain has time to wind down enough for you to get a really good night's sleep. Good quality sleep is really going to help you get through tomorrow and do your best.
5. **Stay calm and relaxed.** Do a mini meditation the night before, the morning before or even between the exams. Meditating will calm you, relax you and reset your mind away from the anxiety and the stress. You could also search for a downloadable mediation audio file to listen to on your phone, or a meditation app. If meditation isn't your thing, do lots of deep breaths, try to go for a brisk walk between the exams and try to keep your mind focused. Don't let people around you stress you out or make you feel inadequate because you've prepared in a different way to them.
6. **Stay focused.** Try to keep your mind focused on the task in hand. Don't think about the next exam, or tomorrow, or next week, or results day. Just think about the question you're answering in the here and now. Just be present in the present and do what you have to do.

Why you get tired after exams

It's very common to feel exhausted and emotionally drained after an exam, particularly when you have more than one exam in a day. And, when you really think about it, it's not hard to understand why you get tired after exams.

First of all, there's the stress of the occasion. In response to the stress of taking an exam, you'll have an adrenaline rush. When you come down from any adrenaline rush you usually feel tired. Your body and your mind have been hyper-stimulated by the fight or flight hormone and now it needs to recharge.

Secondly, there's all the hard work you've done in the lead up to the exam. You've probably been studying harder than you've ever studied in your life. You've kept going on willpower and determination, once the exam is over your body is saying 'enough is enough, we're stopping for a rest now'.

Thirdly, there's the intensity of the exam itself. Exams are an intense and draining experience. I should think that when you're studying or revising you rarely sit, totally focused for longer than an hour. (If you do, you need to change your revision habits and build in breaks to keep you healthy and sane). In exams you could be sitting, 100% focused for up to three hours. You're not used to working at this level of intensity. You pour out everything you've learned over the past years, months and weeks in one intense session; your brain is working hard and your emotions are high because of the stress of the occasion. Of course you're exhausted when it's all over.

So, now you understand why you get tired after exams, how can you manage this tiredness?

- **Plan recovery time** into your revision, if you know you get tired after exams. If you've got day after day of exams, and sometimes two exams on the same day, you need a revision plan where most of your revision is done in advance. Then, you can just 'top-up' your revision the night before each exam.
- **Have a plan for how you're going to recuperate.** Don't just try to force your body and brain to revise when it's screaming at you not to. Have a healthy lunch or snack, sit and watch your favourite programme for an hour and maybe get outside for a walk. You could even take a nap, and then you can get back to work.
- **Make sure you're sleeping well at night.** Have a good bedtime routine that gives you time to wind-down and

relax ready to go to sleep. That includes no computer, phone or tablet screens in the last hour before bed as these give off blue light which sends the wrong signals to your brain about going to sleep. Instead, have a hot bath, read a book or listen to some relaxing music.

It can be really frustrating being tired after exams because you can't get as much revision in as you'd like to. However, instead of fighting it you need to learn to manage it and work with it. This is the most sustainable way to get through exam season.

How to pick yourself up after a bad exam

Sometimes, no matter how prepared you are for an exam, things don't go according to plan. Maybe you misunderstood the question, had a bit of a panic in the middle or just couldn't answer the questions even though you'd practiced really well.

When an exam doesn't go as well as you would have liked it to it can really shake you up emotionally. It can put you off working towards the exams that follow and really undermine your confidence. However, you can't let this happen. Just because one exam hasn't gone well you don't want to compromise your success in all the exams that follow. Here are my tips on picking yourself up after a bad exam.

1. Let the emotion out

It's a horrible feeling when you've done badly at something. Particularly when you've thrown your heart and soul (as well as the kitchen sink) at it. When you suspect you've done badly you need to give your emotions some space to come out.

So, whether you want to sob into your pillow or scream from an isolated hill top, do it. You'll find it very hard to get on with revising for your next exam while you're trying to stifle negative emotions.

2. Pick yourself up again

Once you've let that emotion out you need to pick yourself up, dust yourself off and get back to business. The key here is to remember that one exam is not the be-all and end-all of the exam season.

You've probably got loads of other exams and you really don't want them to go badly too.

So, clear your head and get back to work.

3. Don't keep thinking about it

Once you've let the emotion out the thing is to try to move on. One of my little nuggets of wisdom is that you should **focus on the things you can change and forget the things you can't.**

And when I say don't keep thinking about it that also means stop obsessing over the unofficial mark scheme. In recent years, unofficial mark schemes have been published within hours, and sometimes minutes, of exams finishing. Unofficial mark schemes are not for go-getting action takers. The thing you should remember is that they're unofficial.

The official mark scheme is a working document that is altered and adjusted as the highly experienced markers go through exam papers from thousands of students across the country. There will be a lot of difference between the official and unofficial mark schemes. Only a fool obsesses over something that's rushed out within hours of the exam. But I know you're intelligent, so move on and don't look at it.

4. Try to put right what went wrong

If you can easily identify what went wrong in your bad exam then try and put it right. Maybe you can tell that you didn't do enough past papers. Maybe you know you didn't cover the whole syllabus in your revision. Maybe you know you left your revision too late.

Try and rectify what went wrong as far as you can in the time you've got left before the rest of your exams.

5. Wait until results day to find out how you really did

Do you know what? You might spend the rest of the summer stressing over an exam that you thought went badly but actually be pleasantly surprised by your grade.

Whatever grade you get, it's a total waste of your time and energy to stress over something that you can't change. Try to channel your energy into something more positive and productive, like further reading for your university course.

When you do get your grade you can make informed decisions about what to do next rather than imagining worst-case scenarios and results day Armageddon.

Exam anxiety and positive self-talk

Sometimes, no matter how hard you've worked and how well prepared you are, you're still anxious about exams. Those grades are so important to you that you can't help but turn into a nervous wreck when you think about the exam; your moment of judgement.

There's this voice in your head telling you you're not good enough to get the grade you want and need. It's a mean little voice that mocks your hard work and your ambitions. When you dare to smile with satisfaction because you've done a good revision session or had a great mark back on a past paper it whispers mean words making fun of your pleasure. It's like living with a real-live bully inside your head.

The trouble is, you know from past experience, that even if you do well in past papers you'll freeze when you go into the real exam. It's a combination of the pressure you're putting on yourself and the horrible words of that mean little voice.

You're getting yourself into more and more of a state about how you'll be in your exams as they get closer and closer. You keep doing the work but it doesn't chase away your fears or that bully.

I want you to stop worrying. I'm going to give you some ideas about how to deal with exam anxiety and stand up to that mean little voice. When you practice these techniques your anxiety will ease and your confidence will grow.

Who is that mean little voice?

That mean little voice is your subconscious, and, believe it or not, it's trying to look after you. It's telling you you're not good enough and feeding your fear to try to make you step back from a scary situation. Think back to the cave men and women, who relied on their fear to get themselves out of danger. They relied on these voices in their heads to warn them away from perilous situations.

Exams are hardly equivalent to facing a hungry tiger with your bare hands. But, your body hasn't yet evolved a different, less alarming system to deal with the relative safety of the exam hall compared to the threat of a sabre-toothed tiger.

As far as our society is concerned, exams are important and they're scary. They're also stressful and difficult. There'd be no point in them if they didn't test you to your limits. So, your body reacts the way it would if you were faced with a truly dangerous situation. It warns you off.

How do you deal with that mean little voice?

The first step to dealing with your anxiety and that mean little voice is to acknowledge it, the next thing you must do is thank it. So, the next time you hear it saying, 'what do you think you're doing? You're just wasting your time putting all this work in. You messed up last time, you're definitely going to mess up this time,' you need to talk back to it.

Say something like, 'oh, hello, you. You're trying to protect me again, aren't you? Well thank you for trying to put my best interests first. However, this time I've done the work and I am going to succeed. You can go away now.' Saying this to that mean little voice will send it packing for a little while.

Fill your head with positive thoughts

Once you've sent the little voice away it's up to you to fill your head with positive thoughts that build you up and make you feel confident about the upcoming exams. How do you re-programme your mind like this?

Well, first you have to think about all the negative things you've been telling yourself. Maybe you've been telling yourself that you're rubbish at exams and you always freeze when you go into the exam hall.

What you need to do is find evidence to the contrary. So, if you did really well in one of your mocks that's evidence that you can do well in exam conditions. Create yourself a little phrase or mantra that goes something like this: 'I'm intelligent, capable and hard working. I'm thoroughly prepared for my exams and I keep my head when I sit them.'

If you believe you're unworthy of the grade you want start telling yourself a different story, such as: 'I'm hard working and intelligent. I'm an A grade student.'

If you find it hard to get started with your revision sessions, try this: 'I revise well and productively. My revision brings me excellent results.'

If you find your anxiety over-taking you tell yourself: 'I am calmly and confidently preparing for my exams'.

You get the picture. The key is to contradict the bad things that are going round and round in your head and replace them with good things. If you repeat the good things often enough to yourself you will eventually start to believe them.

The importance of self-talk

Using self-talk, it is possible to re-programme your beliefs about yourself. Don't dismiss these ideas until you've tried them; it's worth it, isn't it, for the sake of achieving your dreams?

How to stop yourself from panicking in exams

Sometimes, even if you've worked hard all year and done the internal work of changing your beliefs about yourself and your mindset, you can still find yourself panicking in exams, although it's much less likely. I'd like to share with you some tips about how to stop the panic when you're actually in the exam hall:

Breathe deeply

When you go into your exam concentrate on breathing deeply. When people are stressed they start breathing rapidly and shallowly. You can trick your body out of feeling stressed if you breathe deeply.

You'll also give yourself something else to think about if you're trying to take really long, deep breaths. Feel your body relax every time you breathe out.

Have exam rituals

Have a little ritual every time you go into an exam. Have you ever watched top tennis players preparing to serve? They always go through the same little routine. They might wipe their face with a towel, take three balls and choose two, put one ball in their pocket and bounce the other a set number of times. They'll then look up at their opponent and go into their service motion.

This ritual tells their body what's coming and helps them to focus. You can have the same kind of thing for exams. For example, taking your watch off and putting it in the top right-hand corner of your desk so you can easily see the time. Placing your pens and pencils where you can easily get them. Straightening the exam paper on your desk and placing your bottle of water on the floor under the right-hand side of the desk. Keeping yourself busy with this little ritual will keep you calm, as well as sending positive signals to your body.

Repeat positive thoughts to yourself

Keep repeating positive mantras or thoughts to yourself. For example, you might keep saying: 'I'm well prepared and capable. I'm going to ace this exam' or, 'I know my stuff. I'm going to do well in this exam.'

Just say something that you can make yourself believe. If negative thoughts try to crowd in instead, just dismiss them and replace them with the positive affirmations.

Keep to time

This is where all that exam technique practice comes into play. You'll have practiced your timings and how to answer every type of question. The thing you have to do is keep to time in your exam. Whenever you see you've got to the end of the time for a question finish your sentence and just move on to the next. If you've filled the allotted time for a question you have had time to write an answer that gets you full marks. You don't want to compromise the next question by not giving it enough time.

Keep your head

If a question comes up that you don't immediately know the answer to, you need to keep your head. These are things that go through my head when I'm not entirely certain how to answer a question:

- What are the key words? Underline them and circle them.
- Make sure I understand the question by reading it through several times.
- What do I know that helps me to answer this question?
- How can I adapt that knowledge to make it answer this question?

I then try to echo back the question to the examiner to show that I'm answering the question but using knowledge that I wouldn't necessarily have picked in a perfect world to help me answer it.

Exam review

Once all your exams are over, it's very tempting to get a really good, long night's sleep and/or to have a great big party to celebrate. However, before too many days have passed it's an excellent idea to spend five or ten minutes reviewing your exam season.

Below are the questions you should be asking when you're reviewing your exam season. Write your answers in the workbook, which you can find at www.lifemoreextraordinary.com/workbook.

1. What went well? What would you do the same next time?

Maybe you used some really good revision techniques that worked for you, you did loads of past exam questions or you really bottomed out the things you didn't understand at the beginning of revision season.

Tip: make a list of all the things that went well and what you'd do the same again next time.

2. What didn't go well? What would you change next time?

Maybe, like 82% of the people who answered a recent *Twitter* poll I did, you feel that you didn't start revising early enough. Maybe you really struggled to maintain your stamina for revision because you didn't take enough revision breaks. Maybe you spent hours in front of your desk feeling like nothing was going in. Write down the things that went badly and how you would change them next time around. If you're stuck for ideas, re-read this book!

Keep your lists of what went well and what you'd change so that next time you have exams you can refer to them and use them to help you to do even better.

That's it! If you follow all this advice you will get the best possible grades you personally are capable of. I wish I could promise you an A* in every subject that you take, but I can't. However, if you follow all my advice you'll know that you've done the very best you can possibly do and you should be deeply satisfied with your effort and results. And, hopefully, you'll be one step closer to achieving the dream you identified in step 1.

"Always dream and shoot higher than you know you can do. Do not bother just to be better than your contemporaries or predecessors. Try to be better than yourself."
William Faulkner

Chapter Summary

- One week before an exam keep up a steady work routine where you continue to focus on your weaknesses, take regular breaks and look after yourself well so you're in peak mental and physical condition for the exam.
- In the last 24 hours before an exam, make sure you're organised, take time to relax and wind down for a good night's sleep and eat a hearty breakfast.
- In the exam hall, slow yourself down to a careful and deliberate speed so that you read all the instructions and questions carefully and accurately. Close your eyes and breathe deeply if you panic. Make sure you answer the question that is written in front of you, not the question you wish was written there, and take time to check your work.
- If you have two exams in one day you need to prepare very thoroughly for both and be prepared to be tired afterwards; exams are emotionally, mentally and physically exhausting.
- If an exam goes badly give yourself time to let out your disappointment but then pick yourself up, dust yourself off and get on with the rest of exam season. One bad exam does not mean that all is lost.
- Get rid of anxiety and nerves with positive self-talk. Reinforce the things you've done well with mantras to build up your confidence and self-belief.
- Once your exams are over take time to review what went well and what didn't go well. This will help you to improve your overall performance next exam season.

References and Acknowledgements

Guise, Stephen. (2013).
Mini Habits: Smaller Habits, Bigger Results. CreateSpace.

Rubin, Gretchen. (2015).
Better Than Before: Mastering the Habits of Our Everyday Lives. Two Roads.

Fowler, F.G. and H.W. (eds) (1988).
The Pocket Oxford Dictionary: Seventh Edition. Oxford.

Oakes, S. and Griffin, M. (2016).
The A Level Mindset: 40 Activities for Transforming Student Commitment, Motivation and Productivity. Crown House.